DATE DUE

The Splendour Falls

The Splendour Falls

The story of the castles of Wales

Wynford Vaughan-Thomas

HTV Cymru/Wales

Published by HTV Cymru/Wales
Television Centre
Cardiff
in association with
Christopher Davies (Publishers) Limited
Rawlings Road, Llandybie, Carms.

First published 1973

SBN 7154 0071 1

Printed in Wales by
Salesbury Press Ltd.
Rawlings Road, Llandybie, Carms.

Contents

Introduction

"The splendour falls on castle walls,
And snowy summits old in story".

So Tennyson wrote in the days of Queen Victoria, but he also expressed the charm and attraction that the old castles of the Middle Ages still have for us in these hurried modern times. Nowhere in these islands does the splendour fall more generously than on the castles of Wales. The Principality must be one of the most "be-castled" parts of Britain.

Only Northumberland and the Scottish Border can rival it. Some of the greater Welsh castles, such as Caernarfon and Caerphilly, are unsurpassed in the whole of Europe. Small wonder, then, that they have become major tourist attractions. The Department of the Environment, which has so many of the castles of Wales in its care, on behalf of the Secretary of State for Wales, estimated that nearly two million people visited them in 1971. The majority of visitors came to the castles built by Edward I along the coast of North Wales, with Caernarfon - the Castle of the Investiture - as the main magnet of attraction. But the lesser-known castles in Mid and South Wales are now becoming increasingly popular. And well do they deserve it.

Is there any castle in Britain with a nobler site than Carreg Cennen in Carmarthenshire, perched on its limestone crag fronting the Black Mountain? Can any give such an impression of impregnable power as Caerphilly, encircled by its wide lake-like moats? Or create such a romantic atmosphere as lonely Castell y Bere, lost in the wilds of Cader Idris? This book is designed to help the visitor to discover the delights of these lesser-known castles of Wales, and also to gain a better understanding of the glories of the greater ones. It is a sequel to the recent successful television series, "The Splendour Falls", first produced in colour on HTV Wales and the West and subsequently shown on the general ITV network.

The visitor to one of the Welsh castles may often be puzzled to understand all he sees. The ruins may be impressive and the surroundings generally romantic and beautiful, but how does he make sense of the complex maze of mysterious passages, broken towers and tumbled walls that lies before him? Was every dark cellar a dungeon? Did the defenders pour molten lead through those strange openings above the gateway, as popular legend demands? Who were the builders of the castles and why were they built when they were? Above all how do they fit into the turbulent but fascinating history of mediaeval Wales, so often totally unfamiliar to people from over the border of the Principality?

This last question seemed to express the main difficulty that confronted the many viewers from all over Britain who wrote to HTV after the televised series of "The Splendour Falls". Welsh History is a special subject not generally taught in schools outside Wales, and the best-informed non-Welsh inquirer can be excused if he finds it difficult to distinguish between Llywelyn ap Gruffydd and Llywelyn ap Iorwerth or fails to unravel the complex rivalries of the sons of the Lord Rhys.

This book is an attempt to fit the castles of Wales into an easily followed outline of Welsh history in the Middle Ages. It does not, of course, claim to make any original contribution to the subject. Its simple aim is to present a summary of the story of the castles of Wales, and of some of the men connected with their building. If the reader can be encouraged further to a deeper reading in this interesting field of study, this will be reward enough for the author.

The main section of the book is therefore historical. We deal very briefly with the beginning of fortification in Wales, with the legacy left by the military engineers of the Roman Army and with the frail attempts at defensive building in the twilight of the Dark Ages. With the advent of the Normans, the castle, as we know it, comes into its own. We trace the stages of the Norman conquests in Wales and show how firmly they were based on castle building. We next show how new techniques were developed in the 12th and 13th centuries, which led eventually to the Concentric Castle, to the triumph of Caerphilly and to the astonishing ring of castles built by Edward I in North Wales. We look at life behind the castle walls and at the accepted methods of attack and defence. Then comes the ever-growing threat of gunpowder. At Raglan we see the castle-builders of Wales making their first attempt to adapt this new force to the whole concept of the mediaeval castle. Finally, we trace the downfall of the castle, its brief, last flicker of life during the Civil Wars and its ultimate ruin. All that remained was the flattery of the 19th century, with its fake baronial reconstructions.

The second section of the book consists of a gazeteer of the chief castles of Wales, a dictionary of technical terms used in describing the parts of a castle, a short glossary of Welsh words likely to be met with when visiting Welsh castles, and some suggestions for further reading on the subject.

An inconsistency will be noticed in the spelling of Welsh place names. Many become anglicised over the ages, or the original Welsh place names were replaced by a completely English one. Thus Abertawe became Swansea, Aberteifi, Cardigan. These original Welsh names are now in process of being restored on maps and road signs. But an English reader might become confused, at this moment of time, if all places were given their correct Welsh title and spelling. He might, for example, find difficulty in detecting Newport under the name of Casnewydd or Builth under Llanfair ym Muallt. Accordingly I have retained names like Laugharne, Neath and the river Towy in their anglicised form, but have placed their correct Welsh name behind them in brackets on their first appearance in the book. Where the correct Welsh spelling does not radically differ from the old anglicised one - as in Caernarfon for Caernarvon-I have preferred the Welsh version. I hope that arrangement will be condoned by the purist and be helpful to the English reader.

Any book of this sort must obviously be based upon the long and patient work of experts in the Welsh historical field, and the list of books at the end of this volume will give some indication of the wide range of their researches. I hope that I have not seriously misinterpreted their findings. I obviously owe a great debt to the Department of the Environment, and have been fortunate during the writing of the "Splendour Falls" in obtaining the help and guidance of Mr. Geraint Walters CBE, lately head of the Department of the Environment in Wales, and of Dr. M.J. Apted, the Chief Inspector of Ancient Monuments of the Department.

I am grateful to them for saving me from many errors.

The Department has now got most of the principal castles of Wales into its capable hands. But for the care of its experts many of our castles would have fallen into complete ruin. In addition, there are admirable Ministry guide books for all the castles in its guardianship.

The present volume aims at a more general view. The author and publisher hope that it will help the reader to appreciate the splendour that still falls from the Castles of Wales.

Cardiff 1973.

1

The First Conquerors

Who were the first people to build fortifications in Wales? Man, the old philosophers maintained, is a quarrelsome animal. We can be sure that the first Welshmen fought and defended themselves from the earliest moment they penetrated into the Welsh hills. But these early Welshmen - if we can call them so, for we have no possibility of discovering what language they spoke - left behind them nothing we can describe as a castle. The first buildings that have survived in Wales are not fortifications but tombs.

You will come across them in lonely, impressive places on the far Preseli Hills of Pembrokeshire, on the winding Menai Straits or on the high ridges of Gower; great slabs of stone, set one upon another, with an engineering skill astonishing in a people who lived some 4,000 years ago. These "cromlechs" are but the bare bones of huge burial chambers, once heaped over with earth or stone. The men who built them were the bearers of a culture which took its inspiration from the rich civilizations developed in the Mediterranean and the great rivers of the Middle East. The world of the ancient hunters was disappearing, and the first farmers had already arrived on our shores. The Neolithic Revolution was in full swing. Man had taken the momentous step from dependence on the chancy business of chasing game to settling down with his flocks of domesticated animals and his small patches of grain. Next came the Bronze Age cairn builders, somewhere around 2,000 B.C. They sailed boldly from headland to headland in search of gold, copper and tin. But did these Neolithic and Bronze Age peoples have any need for elaborate fortifications? They dominated the area we now call Wales for some 4,000 years and it is very hard to believe that all was peace and quiet during this long period of time. Perhaps it was not - there are the remains of what may have been a Neolithic defensive ditch at Castell Bryn-Gwyn, in Anglesey, and a number of recent discoveries by archaeologists suggests that the Bronze Age peoples at least did in fact build some form of simple defences on the hill-tops.

But around 500 B.C. the scene changes dramatically. Bronze gave way before Iron and with iron came the Celts. They came in a series of waves - the high tides of the flood of invaders that poured out from the original Celtic homeland around the Danube basin. And with the Celts, fortification on a big scale came for the first time in Wales.

For the Celts were a warrior race, an aristocracy that delighted in the glamour of battle and whose prowess in combat was ecstatically sung by their bards. Strabo, looking out in the first century A.D., from the safety of the Mediterranean world united under the protection of Rome, could write about the Celts with a fascinated shudder: "The whole nation is war-mad, high-spirited and ready for battle". Classical writers have left vivid descriptions of how the Celts first appeared in the eyes of the Romans; bold men wearing long trousers and cloaks, plastering their hair with lime before battle until it stood out like a lion's mane. Great drinkers - for does not the earliest surviving poem in Welsh, the "Gododdin", record the end of a noble war-band who had unfortunately forgotten to "sign the pledge" before battle and were wiped out almost to a man by the more sober English. But generous to a fault and honouring the artist, be he poet or craftsman. Shields, helmets, weapons were decorated with intricate, flowing designs, for the Celtic mind always thought in curves. The aristocrats fought in chariots. There were special war-bands who came leaping into battle stark naked, since nudity gave magical protection. The Celts gave Wales its first big-scale fortifications - hill forts of all shapes and variety, from the small ramparts on the cliffs of Gower and Pembrokeshire to the vast elaborate earthworks that crown the hills of Glamorgan or the peaks of the Clwydian range. Two of the most impressive can be taken as representative of them all. Behind the little village of Bethlehem in the Towy (Tywi) valley in Carmarthenshire lies the biggest fort in South Wales, Carn Goch. The contrast is strange between the small 19th century chapel in the valley and the ancient heathen ramparts that look down on it. Far away winds the silver Towy and behind, the dark mountains of the Carmarthenshire Vans. Long, broken stone walls enclose over 24 acres. This was not a fort to be permanently occupied. It was a defended village or a place of retreat for a whole tribe in time of trouble, with room for temporary grazing for their animals. Here they could tire out the attackers, who were probably not equipped or organised for a long siege.

Even more impressive is the vast fort of Old Oswestry just over the Welsh border, and one of the finest of the series that lie along the marches of Wales. The original first line of defence was implemented by two extra defensive circles, probably at a time when sling warfare tactics were being introduced from Europe. The entrance winds in among the ramparts, making it easy for the defenders to overwhelm anyone who tried to rush the opening. When you restore, in imagination, the pointed fences and the amazon-like women gathered behind them, screaming their encouragement to the fighting men, you can see that it would require a very well-organised and stout-hearted conqueror to take on the Britons on their home ground. In A.D. 43 the conqueror arrived.

In that year the Romans landed on the coast of Kent. Julius Caesar had, it is true, invaded Britain nearly 100 years before, but his efforts had been large-scale raids designed to teach the bumptious tribes a lesson in the might of Rome. Now the Emperor Claudius ordered a permanent conquest. Britannia was to become an integral part of the empire. In the short space of four years, the legions over-ran lowland Britain. Wales and the North proved far tougher going.

In South Wales the Silures, inhabiting the country between the Wye and the Usk rivers, were the leaders of the resistance. In the north and in central Wales the Ordovices bore the brunt of the fighting. We have vivid descriptions, from great writers like Tacitus, of the sort of battles that marked the long laborious thirty years it took the Romans to conquer Wales. The legions had superb discipline and superior weapons on their side. The Roman soldier was covered by his shield, and after softening the enemy with a salvo of spear-throwing, went in with his short, stabbing sword. The legion moved as one man, an irresistable human battering ram. The British fought more loosely, as individuals, with their princes racing into battle on their war-chariots and leaping from them to rally their men. Inevitably they found, as more primitive people have found after them, that bravery was not enough. When the legions marched against the Ordovices, they produced the same effect as did the English soldiers of the 19th century, armed with rifles and Gatling guns, against the charging Sudanese spearmen at Omdurman.

The Celtic hill-forts would have been formidable to Celtic attackers, but the Romans were masters of the science of siege-craft. Slowly but surely they broke all resistance in Wales. They then covered the country with the usual web of roads, forts and camps in which the Romans always enmeshed the people they conquered. Even so, an undercurrent of unrest continued in Wales. The tribes didn't all go back to their villages and hill-forts to live peacefully under the Pax Romana. The Roman occupation of Wales was a military one.

Only in the South-eastern plains along the Severn do we find the sort of civilian settlement typical of Southern Britain outside the highlands.

Here the showplace is Caerwent (Venta Silurum), a tribal

capital established by the Romans to civilise the conquered Silures - a sort of miniature Roman Cheltenham, complete with public buildings, a shopping centre and, of course, the baths. There was also a scattering of villas in the lowlands of Glamorgan. Over the rest of the country the typical Roman buildings were the military camps of all sizes, connected by a network of roads. The forts could thus be quickly reinforced in case of trouble. The whole system was powered from two great bases, Chester (Deva) in the North, and Caerleon (Isca) in the South. These bases could each accommodate a legion of around 6,000 men. At Caerleon their barracks have been excavated and you can see the walls of the fortress, and the amphitheatre outside the walls built for entertainment or military demonstrations. The legionary soldiers were the élite of the Roman army; tough, well-paid professionals, for whom fighting was a full-time career. The general atmosphere of Caerleon or Chester would be familiar to anyone who remembers the old British army bases in India or the Far East, down to the swarms of traders settled outside the gates!

Out from the bases radiated the great military roads. At strategic points on them were built the auxiliary forts, constructed to a standardised pattern. They were generally in the shape of a playing card and protected by a rampart of earth faced with stone, later strengthened by a stone parapet and stone turrets at intervals. Inside the fort, the barracks and administrative buildings were laid out on a regular pattern. An average fort might cover about five acres.

These smaller forts would be garrisoned by auxiliary troops, many of them recruited from far-off parts of the empire. I have often wondered how the Spaniards stationed at Brecon, or the men from France who garrisoned the fort near Bala, felt when they turned out for duty on a cold, drizzling dawn in the damp Welsh winter! Some of these camps and forts were placed on extremely bleak and lonely places, like Y Pigwn on top of the hills around the source of the Usk, or Tomen-y-Mur above the wild moorlands of Trawsfynydd.

A good idea of what these forts must have looked like in their hey-day can be obtained at Cardiff. The Third Marquess of Bute was an extremely wealthy nobleman with a passion for the past. In late Victorian times he reconstructed the eastern and northern walls of this 4th century fortress on the base of the original walls. These still survive, hidden or incorporated in the re-construction. The result is impressive. You can see why the Celtic tribesmen must have looked on a place like Cardiff with awe, if not with affection. They could build hill-forts, but nothing so regular, orderly and powerful as a great Roman fortress.

So the unshakeable grid of Roman roads and forts held Wales in its grip for over 300 years. The natives didn't altogether abandon their original settlements. Traces of occupation in Roman times have been found in many of the old hill-forts. At Tre'r Ceiri in Caernarvonshire, high on one of the sharp-pointed summits of the mountain group of the Rivals, lies a whole small town of circular and winding defences, inhabited from the first to the fourth century. This unplanned clutter of buildings stands in strong contrast to the disciplined order of the great Roman fort at Caernarfon (Segontium), not ten miles away. To the inhabitants of Tre'r Ceiri, Segontium must have looked impregnable - part of the permanent, irremovable order of things.

Then unbelievably, the solid structure of the Roman Empire began to crack. Historians still argue why. A failure of will at the centre, financial troubles, increasing pressure of the barbarian tribes from the outside? All may have played their part in this world-shaking set-back of civilisation. Wales, on the perimeter of the Empire, was bound to be among the first provinces to feel the effects. The neighbouring island of Ireland had never come under the yoke of the Roman army. Now it became a fountainhead of raiders closing in on an ailing Rome. You can see the signs of anxiety in the measures taken by the military authorities to protect Wales. The fort at Cardiff was enlarged and may have been the headquarters of a fleet. A new coastal fortification was built at Holyhead, whose walls can still be seen forming the boundaries of the churchyard. At Caernarfon the remains of a fortified warehouse and landing-place stand among the modern villas of South Road, overlooking the

PEMBROKE. The springboard for the invasion of Ireland.

KIDWELLY. The marcher lords controlled the church and the castle.

River Seiont. No doubt other third century fortlets and signal stations were established along·the coast. For the seashores of the west had suddenly become dangerous. Even the peaceful citizens of Caerwent, who must have thought of themselves as part of the settled Empire, felt compelled to strengthen the defences around their little town and then add a series of bastions to it. The wall still stands - one of the most impressive remains of Roman rule above ground in Wales, but also one of the most tragic. When a bastion of the south wall was cleared during the modern excavations, it contained human skeletons and skulls, no doubt thrown there after a barbarian raid. Darkness was, indeed, settling over the land.

A last gleam fell over Caernarfon. In 383 A.D. Magnus Maximus persuaded the troops in Britain to join him in a bid for the imperial throne. He probably drained Wales of its last reserves of professional soldiers. He had four years of dazzling success until he was finally beaten and killed by Theodosius at Aquileia. But he left a story that haunted the imagination of the Welsh throughout the Dark Ages that followed. They called him Macsen Wledig who married a British princess, "Helen of the Legions". They declared that he had lived in the golden castle of Caernarfon and only left it for the greater glory of ruling the whole, wide world from Rome.

The Romans left behind them legends and dreams of glory but, curiously enough, the Welsh felt no need to inherit their skill in the art of fortification. They borrowed plenty of Latin words for military matters. In Welsh, the term for a wall is "mur" (murum) and for ditch "ffos" (fossa). Other borrowings are "ffenestr" from "fenestra" - a window, "pont" from "pontus" - a bridge, and the very word for a castle from Latin "castra", in Welsh "castell". But for many, many years to come no one in Wales would build a castle or any fortification on a big scale. No-one could command the organisational power to do so.

In the fifth century all vestiges of Roman rule seemed to have collapsed in Wales. Barbarian pressure grew on all sides. On the eastern seaboard of Britain, the Saxon pirates closed in and drove their settlements ever further westward. The Scotti, from Ireland, descended in hordes, in the skin boats so vividly described by Gildas, the learned if somewhat querulous monk who has left us the only written account of these times:

"Their hulls might be seen creeping across the glassy surface of the main like so many insects awakened from torpor by the heat of the noonday sun and making with one accord for some familiar haunt." The Britons from the lowland areas of these islands may have yielded to the pressure, but the Western Britons struggled to acquit themselves like men. If they had not, Wales would never have emerged from the darkness.

Was there some great leader who rallied the western British and helped them check the barbarian onrush? Immediately we come up against the Problem of Arthur. No figure has haunted the imagination of the Welsh, and indeed the whole of Britain, more completely than that of noble King Arthur, with his band of glittering Knights of the Round Table. If the final touches to his fame were added by the French romancers of the High Middle Ages, and transmitted later by Sir Thomas Malory, there can be no question that the author who first launched Arthur on his astonishing career was the great mystery-man of mediaeval literature, Geoffrey of Monmouth. No matter where Geoffrey got his material for his History of the Kings of Britain, he immediately became the best-seller of the twelfth century. For Geoffrey was a great literary artist. He told of King Lear, of Lud who built London; of Cymbeline; of the giants Gog and Magog and of a whole host of other dubious heroes that have become so fixed in our minds that we find it hard to believe that they were all invented by the ingenious Geoffrey. But his greatest success was King Arthur and his councillor, the wizard, Merlin, who ruled Britain from his capital of Caerleon or Camelot. Europe avidly swallowed every detail of Geoffrey's story.

Wales honoured the great King Arthur by attaching his

name to every available site. There were Arthur's seats, Arthur's stones, Arthur's castles scattered all over the land. Modern historians have not dismissed the existence of some sort of Arthur. Maybe he was the leader of a powerful war-band of professional fighters who formed the nucleus of the resistance. And he could well have been the general who gained the great victory of Mount Badon around 500 A.C., which checked the Saxon advance to the west. What is quite certain, however, is that he could not have lived in the glorious fortresses and castles described with such loving gusto by Geoffrey of Monmouth and Sir Thomas Malory. These romantic Camelot-worthy edifices certainly never existed in Wales.

The truth is somewhat different. When Wales emerges from the mists in the early sixth century, we see a land split into a series of small kingdoms, each ruled by a prince settled in strongholds scattered over the country. Arthur - or the Arthur-figure and his war-band - had held off the English advance on a line that certainly lay well east of the Severn. He had given the Celtic world a breathing space, a chance of an Indian summer before the ultimate darkness of the Dark Ages.

This was the hey-day of the Saints - of the learned St. Illtud who made his monastery at Llantwit Major in Glamorgan a centre of scholarship that keep alight the torch of classical learning in a rough and threatening world; of the ascetic St. David, whose austerities and sweetness of character so impressed his countrymen that they made him their patron saint. Christian Wales thus felt itself the defender of civilisation against the barbarians who had overrun eastern Britain. The Kinglets of Wales still inscribed their gravestones in Latin, even if that Latin was touchingly uncertain.

We get a glimpse of their way of life in three sites, fortified in the Dark Ages, that have been carefully excavated in recent years. The most romantic of these sites is Dinas Emrys in Caernarvonshire. As you drive up from Beddgelert towards the inner fastnesses of Snowdonia you pass through the wildly beautiful Vale of Gwynant - a landscape of heather-covered crags, lakes and woods, with the great peaks of Eryri guarding the sky-line. A high rock rises from the centre of the vale to be mirrored in the still waters of Llyn Dinas. If you climb up through the tangles of dwarf-oaks that cover the sides of the crag, you come across the equally tangled lines of broken, low walls that mark the summit. From the earliest days Welsh tradition has connected these humble vestiges with the long past glories of the Age of Arthur.

To this lonely rock, the old legends maintain, fled the great Vortigern, once the all-powerful ruler of Britain. He had betrayed the island by paying the false Saxons to fight for him as mercenaries. The mercenaries stayed, invited their friends and allies to join them, and soon had the whole of lowland Britain in flames and confusion. Vortigern took refuge in the mountains of Wales and set about building his last stronghold on Dinas Emrys. But a mysterious force defied his efforts. No matter how high the walls were built during the day, they were tumbled to the ground during the night. Vortigern consulted his magicians. They declared that the only way of building up the castle in peace was to find a boy who had been born without a father, sacrifice him on the summit of the crag and sprinkle his blood on the stones. This curious boy was eventually found in South Wales. His name was Emrys, the Welsh version of the Latin Ambrosius. But when he was brought before Vortigern he proved to be a far better wizard than those on whom Vortigern had relied.

Far below the foundations, he declared, lay a lake, and at the bottom of the lake, a pavilion in which two great dragons were fighting. One was white representing the Saxons, and the other red representing the Welsh. Their terrible struggle shook down the walls every night. Vortigern ordered a well to be dug, and lo and behold! everything Emrys said proved to be true. The two dragons rose into the air and in the battle that followed, the red dragon beat the white. Thus the ultimate survival of Wales was assured! To Dinas Emrys, later on, came Uther Pendragon, the father of King Arthur himself.

So the legends gathered. In 1954-56, Dr. Hubert Savory of

the National Museum of Wales carefully explored the site. It was impossible, of course, to tell if Vortigern or Ambrosius had ever lived there and there was no sign of the dragons! But Dr. Savory uncovered traces of a great hall and a building nearby which could have been a storehouse or was used by slaves. Whoever lived at Dinas Emrys in the Dark Ages was no barbarian. He was a ruler who enjoyed some degree of wealth and luxury.

The same may be said of two other sites in Wales, both excavated in recent years by Dr. Leslie Alcock. One is also in the north, this time on the coast at the mouth of the Conway estuary. A rocky hill with twin summits rises behind the township of Deganwy. These summits again give splendid views across the widening river to Conway and the great mountains of the Carneddau beyond. A place made by Nature for a royal residence. Again the legends gathered.

Here, they say, lived the powerful prince named Maelgwn Gwynydd. He is one of the rulers denounced by Gildas in some of the most blistering pages of "De Exidio Brit-anniae". According to Gildas, Maelgwn had usurped the throne, oppressed the church, listened to the flattery of his bards and murdered his wife. But even Gildas admitted that Maelgwn had nobility, courage and was a generous giver. Popular stories credited him with cunning and resource. Maelgwn, according to legend, was one of the four rulers of Wales who met at the estuary of the Dovey to decide who should be the Brenin Pennaf, or the chief King. They agreed to a Canute-like test. They would all sit on their thrones fronting the incoming tide. He who stayed longest on his throne would be acknowledged as the supreme King. Mael-gwn cunningly fitted his throne with some sort of secret water-wings. His three rivals were overthrown by the tide while he floated happily above the flood. Thus he became the chief ruler of Wales, and certainly the one man who stands out as a real person at the onset of the Dark Ages. We also have a possible date for his death. A great plague swept Europe in 547 A.D. and Maelgwn, we are told, fled from it to the safety of a church near Deganwy. But he saw the plague through the keyhole of the door in the form of a fearsome Yellow Beast. And so he died.

If you climb the hill at Deganwy you will come across traces of the foundations of a far later castle, built by Henry III. Maelgwn's citadel probably occupied the highest of the twin crags. You need to be an expert to detect the fifth and sixth century walls from the rest of the tumbled stones, but, as at Dinas Emrys, there is a spirit about the place which seems to take you far back into the Dark Ages.

The third site that has thrown light on this obscure, strange period in our history lies in South Wales. Recent excavations at Dinas Powis, a few miles south-west of Cardiff, have disclosed that the place was the residence of a fifth or sixth century princeling, who lived in a certain amount of wealth and luxury and whose great hall and surrounding buildings were defended by a ditch and a palisade. As at Dinas Emrys and Deganwy those defences are comparatively modest compared to the Roman forts and the big hillforts of the Celts in the Iron Age. Nor will they compare with the fortifications built later on by the Normans. These are not castles but rather fortified dwelling houses. The way of life they represent did not need the elaborate defences of the true castle. Warfare was not a series of sieges of fortified positions. The earliest Welsh heroic poetry of Aneirin and Taliesin, dating back to the sixth century, show us the chieftain, secure in his great hall surrounded by his war-band of faithful retainers. Warfare was open and mobile with mounted troops playing an important part. It is significant that the first mention in the Welsh annals of an attack on a fortified place does not occur until 1093, by which time the Normans were firmly in the picture. Until they arrived, no one in Wales felt the need to build a castle.

Away in the west, in what was the old kingdom of Dyfed and is now modern Pembrokeshire, you come across a series of small circular earthworks which may represent the defences around the dwelling-places of a chief, rather like the "raths" of ancient Ireland. Some of these may have been first constructed even before the Romans came to Wales, but it seems likely that excavation in the future will confirm that occupation continued into the Dark Ages. Meantime, the darkness increased. After the respite gained by the Arthurian victories, the Saxon advance was resumed. The Welsh were isolated from their Celtic countrymen in the north and in Cornwall. Slowly they were pushed westward towards their refuge in the mountain-keep of the hills. Here the Welsh held on to the last, desperately, doggedly and successfully.

Their success is symbolised, in a curious way, by one of the most impressive earthworks in the whole of Britain - Offa's Dyke. It can be traced from the coast of North Wales at Prestatyn down to the mouth of the River Wye in the south. It is not continuous and maybe the sections across the heavily wooded Herefordshire plains were not needed and so were never constructed, or they may have consisted of little more than a timber palisade of which no trace now survives. But in the hill country of the marches of mid-Wales, you can see the Dyke splendidly displayed. It seems to writhe over the landscape like some monstrous snake. There can be no question that it was built under the order of Offa, the great King of Mercia in the English midlands, who died in 795 A.D. What was its purpose? The deep ditch of the dyke lies on the Welsh side but clearly it was not intended to be a constantly manned defence line like Hadrian's Wall. It was an attempt to mark the boundary for all time, with some agreement, under force, from the Welsh. The modern boundary rarely coincides with it, but it has remained the emotional boundary of Wales. To this day Welshmen speak of going to live in England as "crossing Offa's Dyke".

Place names indicate its effectiveness. On one side you find the Welsh "Tre's" and "Llan's", on the other the English "hams" and "tons". No doubt it was an effective obstacle to large-scale cattle raids, but the story that any Welshman found on the wrong side was legally bound to have his right hand cut off was a later invention.

Offa's Dyke is the greatest of the earthwork boundaries in Wales, but there are one or two others which deserve attention. Up in the north, in Flintshire, a second dyke, Wat's Dyke, can be traced a few miles to the east and roughly parallel to Offa's Dyke. The reason for its construction is not clear. It might have been a rehearsal for the more formidable barrier of Offa's Dyke, marking an earlier stage of English conquest. In South West Wales a mysterious earthwork, Ciawdd Mawr, lies on the moorland at the headwaters of the Gwili river. It can be seen crowning the westward slopes of the valley as you drive up the road from the little village of Conwyl Elvet, through Cwm-Duad on the road towards Llandysul. It cannot be traced for more than a few miles but it may have been designed to be a barrier on the neck of the mountainland that separates the valley of the Tywi from that of the Teifi. Its date is equally conjectural. Was it the boundary of the old kingdom of Dyfed back in the 6th century? In any case, it is a small affair compared with the great dyke built by Offa.

Offa's Dyke worked both ways. If it penned in the Welsh among their wild hills, it also allowed them to consolidate their position in safety. The 9th century saw Wales united politically for the first time since the days of the Romans. Under the powerful leadership of Rhodri the Great the Welsh succeeded in driving off the Viking raiders. Rhodri became king of the whole country and earned the thanks of no less a ruler than Charles the Great for his bravery in facing the menace of the Viking. Rhodri's grandson, Hywel the Good (Hywel Dda) was, according to tradition, the first man to codify the laws of Wales, and became the ally and friend of the great rulers of the English kingdom of Wessex. Wales, at the beginning of the 10th century, seemed set fair to create a strong, independent kingdom under a powerful ruling family. Yet, in the period between the death of Hywel Dda around 950 A.D. and the advent of the Normans, the scene sadly changes. Wales falls into confusion. The title of supreme overlord is fiercely disputed. The country is split into smaller kingdoms, usually torn by feuds over a disputed succession. Sometimes a bold, daring figure such as Gruffydd ap Llywelyn, the Lord of Gwynedd, reimposed unity but the seeds of disintegration were always there. Maybe the very geography of the country had something to do with it; all the most fertile tracts of land are separated by wild mountain ranges. Or again, estates were too often weakened by the custom of equally dividing inheritances. But the over-riding factor was the presence in the background of the united powerful English state, whose rulers had no desire to see an equally united Wales on their doorstep. The Welsh could never conduct their politics in isolation.

Thus Wales stood in the eventful year of 1066, when William the Norman landed at Pevensey to change the face of history in England. With him came his barons and above all his skilful craftsmen, experts in the art of castle-building. For the first time we meet the genuine castle as distinct from the hill-forts, the Roman forts and the defended dwelling-place we have been discussing so far. And the castle was to change, not only English history, but the history of Wales as well.

2

The Coming of the Normans

The Welsh took no part in the Battle of Hastings. Indeed, most of them may never have heard of it; and those who did may even have rejoiced that Harold and his Anglo-Saxon haus-carls had been so completely overwhelmed by William and his mounted knights. For Harold had been a sore trial to the Welsh along the Border. He had even crushed the redoubtable Gruffydd ap Llywelyn, whose head was sent to him as the price of peace. Harold had now fallen in his turn. Maybe the Welsh could, as in the past, turn the troubles of England to their advantage. If they thought so, they were soon bitterly undeceived. The men who now arrived on the Welsh border were the toughest warriors and the most brilliant organisers in the Europe of their time.

The Normans were the descendants of the Vikings who had settled in Northern France during the great raids of the 8th and 9th century. They made a deal with the French rulers, and rapidly assimilated the manner and techniques of all that was forward-looking in contemporary Europe. This, coupled with the restless, adventurous spirit of their Norse ancestors, made them formidable foes. William over-ran England in a few years. The Anglo-Saxons had already created a centralised administration which the Conqueror could take over. There would be revolts, riots, rebellions, but William was there in the centre ready to smash them with his strong mailed horsemen, and hold the English down with his castles. Wales was another matter.

The Normans reached the borders of Wales very soon after the defeat of the English at Hastings. In fact, there had been some Normans on parts of the border even before William the Conqueror's invasion. They had settled in Herefordshire and obviously must have built strongholds of some kind.

We hear of Richard, son of Scrob, constructing one a few miles south of Ludlow, and of Osbern Pentecost who may have built the first castle at Ewias Harold. The Welsh under Gruffyd ap Llywelyn had dealt summarily with them. But now the Normans had arrived in force along the whole length of the border.

Here they were facing a different people, but above all a different landscape. An advance into mountainous Wales was bound to be a slower business than the over-running of lowland England. William soon realised that his first priority, in the years that followed Hastings, was thoroughly to establish his authority in the richest part of his new conquest. He had perforce to leave the subjugation of the Welsh, or at least the pinning them into the bleaker parts of their mountains, to certain of his great subjects.

As these powerful barons conquered Welsh lands and dispossessed the original Welsh rulers, they also assumed the legal rights and powers of the men whose places they took. Power in Wales had always been broken down into smaller, more localised units than in semi-centralized England and heavily centralized Normandy. The new owners were thus able to assume rights in Wales which would never have been countenanced in England. William and his successors did not approve. No Norman King ever gave away even a tiny portion of power except under pressure. For the moment, the pressure of events in England forced them to turn a blind eye to some of the things that were going on in the new frontier society that was growing up along the Welsh border.

We are now in the presence of the Lords Marcher, men with private armies and private justice who were to have a powerful influence not only on Welsh but on English history through the Middle Ages. The March derives from an old French word meaning the "border". The Lords Marcher were the bold barons of the borderland whose rights far exceeded those of their brethren in England. They were the people who now proceeded to turn their technique of castle-building to the conquest of Wales.

In the north, Hugh of Avranches, a cruel rapacious man, pushed along the North Wales coast from Chester. In Mid-Wales, Roger of Montgomery advanced into the valley of the upper Severn from his base at Shrewsbury. In South Wales, William Fitzosbern proved to be one of the most successful of the border barons. He was the Conqueror's cousin and quickly established his position as Earl of Hereford. He seized the lower Wye Valley, and from his stronghold of Chepstow, conquered the land of Gwent between the Wye and the Usk. These men had two great advantages over their Welsh opponents. They commanded bodies of armoured horsemen, the panzer divisions of their day; and they knew how to build castles.

The technique of their advance was soon standardized. The armed men and their followers would push their way up wide valleys and along the coast, and their advances might follow the line of the old Roman roads. The lightly-armed Welsh might harrass or ambush them, but as long as they kept to the lower valleys and stayed away from the higher hills, the mailed Norman knights could always get through to some strategic point. Here they constructed a castle.

The Welsh, or for that matter the English, were not alone in finding these Norman military techniques impossible to cope with. Similar methods swept the Normans to spectacular conquests in Spain, in Sicily, in Eastern Europe and, eventually, the Holy Land. The Norman knight on horseback in his coat of mail, with his sword, conical helmet and kite-shaped shield, became the champion warrior of the Western World. A concerted charge by even a small number of these highly trained Norman knights was widely held to be irresistible. In the vivid words of Anna Comnena, the learned daughter of the Emperor of Byzantium who observed the Normans at close quarters during the 2nd Crusade, the crunch of a Norman charge "might make a hole in the walls of Babylon." Of course, the knights needed their following of archers and foot-soldiers, but the concentrated impact of a band of mailed knights was the Norman's real 'secret weapon'.

It is curious to discover how recent a thing in the history of Europe was this charge of trained horsemen. It would not have been possible but for an important invention which transformed the business of war at the dawn of the Middle Ages. This was the stirrup. It seems incredible that this simple and vital piece of equipment was so late in arriving on the military scene. In the Parthenon frieze in the British Museum, the young Athenian knights are depicted controlling their horses purely by knee pressure. The same thing occurs in all the battle scenes on the triumphal arches and columns of the Romans. These riders would have been wobbly and insecure in a real battle clash. The Legion, with which the Romans conquered the Western World, was a disciplined infantry formation. It operated against less heavily armoured enemies like the Celts, and had proved irresistible. Cavalry, to Roman military thinkers, were always an auxiliary force. This may have held back the development of true cavalry tactics. But sometime about the middle of the 7th century, the Muslim armies had introduced the use of the stirrup, maybe following the example of China. From the Muslims it passed into the Christian armies of the West. It s effect was revolutionary.

If a rider sat in a saddle with a high pommel and cantle, and put his feet firmly into stirrups, he formed almost a single unit with his horse. If he then couched a long, heavy lance under his right arm and rode hard at his foe, he could strike not only with his own force but with the strength of his war-horse as well. The shock impact of even a small group of properly equipped horsemen upon more lightly armed foot-soldiers would be shattering.

It accounts for many of the surprising victories of small bands of Normans against more numerous opponents in the early days of the Norman advance into Wales.

It so happens that we have an eye-witness account of one such charge carried out in conjunction with the defence of a castle - an interesting example of the combination of the two military arts in which the Normans excelled. The account comes from the year 1116 when the Normans had already pushed deep into West Wales and had constructed their primitive castles in North Cardiganshire; but this scene must have already been repeated on many an occasion during the earlier Norman advance. The chronicler of the monastery of Llanbadarn just outside the modern Aberystwyth watched a large army of Welshmen under their leader, the returned exile Gruffydd ap Rhys, advancing to attack the castle of Ystrad Antaron. This was built on the far side of the river Ystwyth, and was reached by a wooden bridge. Gruffydd had attracted a motley force to his banner. The Welsh had already met with considerable success in their attacks on some of the new Norman castles in the Towy, (Tywi) and Teifi valleys. Now they marched westwards. That night they swept the country clear of supplies, including some cattle belonging to the monastery. The chronicler is careful to point out that this sacrilegious act brought its swift retribution. During the night, Razo, the Norman castellian, received reinforcements. Gruffydd's horde advanced, confident of victory. Razo lured them across the the bridge by a galling fire from his archers. When he had got the Welsh between the castle and the river, he launched his small band of mailed horsemen in a shock charge. The Welsh attack immediately collapsed. Once again, the trained mail-armoured man on the horse had beaten the undisciplined warrior on foot. It is also intriguing to note that not all the Normans operating in Wales rejoiced in noble names like William Fitosbern or Maurice de Londres. These second-rank followers of the greater lords sound tougher and more familiar under names like Razo and Richard, son of Scrob!

But Razo's castle would not for a moment have resembled the elaborate stone structures, complete with towers, keeps

The Castle of Dôl, from the Bayeux Tapestry.

and inner and outer wards, that we associate with the word 'castle' today.

It would have been of the type known as a "motte and bailey". The bailey was an enclosure, formed by a high bank of earth surrounded by a ditch and topped with a strong wooden palisades. This enclosure would be big enough to contain a hall, stables, a well, workshops for the smith or the armourer, a storehouse and, if possible, a chapel - for the Normans always believed that the sword would cut more keenly if there was a prayer behind it. Attached to the bailey was a high mound or "motte", on which was perched a watch-tower or a final keep, a strong-point if the enemy broke into the bailey. In the early days of the Norman advance, the whole structure of the "motte and bailey" would be of earth and wood. You can see what it was like from that earliest and most vivid of strip cartoons, the Bayeux Tapestry.

This famous piece of embroidery depicts the events leading up to Hastings and the great battle itself. We see the Normans building a castle as soon as they land, with the men hard at work throwing up the high mound. An army could mobilise enough man-power to create quite a respectable mound in a few days, but the smaller bands who conducted the penetration into the Welsh border-land would have taken some weeks to construct their "motte". On the top of the "motte", a wooden tower would be built. Again you can see one depicted in the Bayeux Tapestry - that at Dol. This is a lightly Chinese-pagoda-looking tower, with Duke Conan nonchalantly sliding down a rope to escape the unwelcome attentions of William the Conqueror.

These "motte and bailey" mounds can be found in large numbers along the whole length of the Welsh borders, in the coastal lands of South Wales and in Pembrokeshire. Not every mound you can see belongs to the period of the Conquest. This technique of defence was a most convenient one and it continued to be employed in the perpetual warfare against the Welsh for well over a hundred and fifty years after 1066. Its origin is still disputed by historians. It may have begun in the low-lying country around the mouths of the Rhine. But, even if it wasn't adopted in many other parts of Europe, it certainly suited Welsh conditions. You come across an astonishing number of these mottes in Monmouthshire and Radnorshire. Some of the most romantically placed of them lie along the road from Knighton as it climbs over the outlying hills of the Radnor Forest into Central Wales. At the summit of the pass is the motte and bailey of Craig Eryr. It would be difficult to find a more evocative site.

Like so many other aspects of castle-building, the earliest of the Norman castles in Wales were not completely standardised. There were several variants on the simple motte and bailey structure. The motte could be sited in the centre of the circle of the bailey. Or it might be dispensed with altogether. The defence would then consist simply of a ringwork protected by a deep ditch. This seems to have been the variant followed by the Normans as they pushed into the Gower peninsula at the beginning of the 12th century. The ramparts of the old circular fort at Penrice are still visible, although with difficulty, for the site is now heavily overgrown and is not easy of access from the road. More rewarding is Penmaen Old Castle, magnificently placed on a headland looking down over the limestone cliffs and golden sands of Three Cliffs Bay. Recent excavations have shown that the circular rampart was composed of a massive bank of limestone rubble. The gate-tower was of wood and had clearly been burnt during one of the many raids made by the Welsh into Gower during the early days of the Norman occupation. The site was abandoned some time before the mid-13th century and was never occupied by a later stone castle.

On other sites in Wales the builders were content with the motte and left out the bailey altogether.

Occasionally the advancing Normans found use for the ruins of some of the old Roman forts. They flung up a mound at one of the corners of the wall at Caerwent, and again at Caerleon. Needless to say the mound at Caerleon, in the true spirit of Geoffrey of Monmouth, was later confidently pointed out as the site of King Arthur's Round Table.

When William Rufus made his great foray into Wales in 1095 he used the old Roman fort at Trawsfynydd as one of his defence points, and the high mound he constructed gives its name to the place - Tomen y Mur - "the mound of the wall". It now looks down on the far higher walls of the Atomic Power Station and on the wide lake of Trawsfynydd.

The highest mound in Wales is one of the most accessible. It stands in the middle of Cardiff Castle. Again the Normans took advantage of the Roman fort to create the "bailey", and threw up the mound in the centre of it. Later on, the wooden palisade or tower on the original mound was replaced by a circle of stone walling to form a "shell-keep", one of the finest examples in Britain. However it was used, the motte at Cardiff was a formidable proposition. It must have intimidated the Welsh. No wonder that, during the reign of William Rufus, the Marcher Barons swept deep into Wales. With their technique of quick castle-building and their irresistible armour, they seemed certain to overwhelm the Welsh resistance. In the North, they had reached Anglesey. In the centre, they had crossed the wild mountains of Plynlimon and were edging along the shores of Cardigan Bay. A Norman castle went up at Cardigan, and from this base the invaders poured south into Dyfed. They built the first castle at Pembroke; a rough stockade, but placed on a position of great natural strength.

Pembroke had the remarkable record of being the only castle in Wales which never fell, even temporarily, into the hands of the Welsh. It was, however, captured, in its extreme old age, by none other than Oliver Cromwell! By that time gunpowder had much reduced the defensive power of the mediaeval castle.

The Normans were also advancing into the valley of the Usk. In Glamorgan, Robert Fitzhamon, using his new castle of Cardiff and its great motte as his base, led the conquest of the rich plain lands of the Vale of Glamorgan which were, thereafter, forever lost to the Welsh. Around this conquest of Glamorgan a whole mass of picturesque stories has gathered. Fitzhamon is supposed to have had twelve knights with

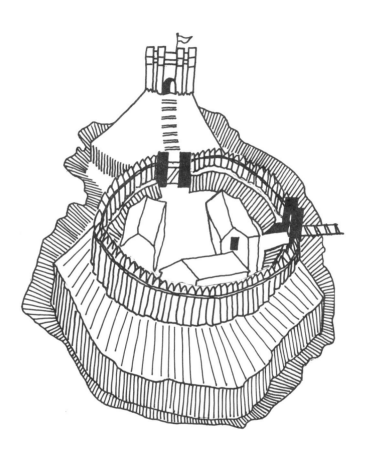

A Motte and Bailey

whom he shared his loot. One of them, Payn de Turbeville, cornered a leading Welsh prince named Morgan in his stronghold at Coity, near Bridgend. Confronted by Payn's men-at-arms, Morgan appeared, leading his daughter by one hand and carrying a naked sword in the other. "I am old," he said to Payn, "if you marry my daughter, you will have all my lands without bloodshed when I die. If you refuse, we will fight to the last drop of our blood." Payn naturally accepted the offer, although History does not relate if the maiden was as desirable as the castle.

In fact, History does not relate anything about this remarkable encounter between Morgan and Payn, although Payn himself is real enough and his family subsequently played a distinguished part in the annals of Glamorgan. But the Coity story (and many other similar delightful stories about the conquest) seems to have originated in Tudor times, when the new Tudor nobility were anxious to lend a little antique distinction to their parvenu families.

But no matter what happened in Glamorgan, the spectacular first onrush of the Normans into Wales was bound to provoke a violent reaction. Suddenly, the Welsh struck back. The whole country was aflame with revolt. The new castles, which must have been of the "motte and bailey" type, were burnt and levelled. In North and Central Wales the check was decisive. Certainly Gwynedd would remain a solid bastion of Welsh independence for nearly two hundred years, while Powyd, by cunning as much as by war, kept Central Wales Welsh for a similar period. Only in South Wales could the Normans claim to have held their original gains. Here indeed, they made them permanent; especially when the masterful, tireless Henry I succeeded Rufus and took a special interest in Wales. All along the Southern coasts, colonies of English were established. They settled in the Vale of Glamorgan and in Southern Gower. In Southern Pembrokeshire, Fleming immigrants formed a powerful element in the population; the winding reaches of Milford Haven allowed the settlers to penetrate far inland. Southern Pembrokeshire became "Little England beyond

Wales", with the boundary between the races marked to this day by the "Landsker".

In this new climate of consolidation, something far more solid was needed in the way of castles than the "motte and bailey".

The weakness of the motte and bailey against a foe who was now better organised and armed was strikingly illustrated in the celebrated story of the abduction of Nest, the wife of Gerald of Windsor by Owain, the son of the Prince of Powys. In 1109, Gerald was the custodian of the first castle of Pembroke. The beauty of his wife had become a legend throughout the country. The brave and dashing Owain attended a feast given by his father on his lands in Cardiganshire, and heard the bards singing the praises of "the Helen of Wales". He determined to see for himself if the beauty of Nest lived up to the bardic eulogies. He discovered that Gerald and his wife were then visiting the castle of Cenarth Bychan, which is usually identified with the present site of Cilgerran, although there is no certainty in this matter. It is pleasant to suppose, however, that here on the noble crag that rises above the wooded gorge of the river Teifi, Owain gazed on Nest and fell madly in love with her. Like Paris, in Homer's story, he seems also to have found favour in the eyes of Nest. Owain determined to abduct her. On a dark night a few days later, he returned to Cenarth Bychan with fifteen determined companions. They burrowed under the threshold of the gate, rushed in on the sleeping household, placed a guard on the bedroom of Nest and then added to the confusion by setting the rest of the castle on fire. Gerald de Windsor escaped through the unromantic exit of the "garderobe" - in other words the latrine. Owain carried off Nest and her children and began a war which set the whole of Wales in an uproar. In spite of frequent periods of exile in Ireland, Owain eventually succeeded his father as Prince of Powys, and made a reasonably successful one as well. He even regained the favour of Henry I. But Gerald de Windsor had never forgotten the abduction of Nest. At the height of his success, Owain was lured into an ambush and slain by the Flemings of Pembrokeshire. At last Gerald was avenged.

This tale is typical of the wild, reckless and turbulent life men lived in those days on the Welsh-Norman borderland, but the castle student will immediately note that Owain and his companions were able to burrow under the threshold of the door of Cenarth Bychan castle with comparative ease. They were also able to set most of the castle on fire in a matter of minutes. Clearly the Cilgerran of that time - if it was Cilgerran - was not the imposing, stone built castle we see here today. It must have been a motte and bailey affair, and the buildings of the bailey and the surrounding palisades must have been of wood. Fire was always the great danger in this type of castle. We can also note that there was another weak point - the doorway. The lesson of attacks like those of Owain were not lost upon the castle builders. In one or two strategic centres in South Wales, fortifications of extremely solid stone now started to rise. At last we begin to see the familiar shape of the true Norman castle.

The Normans had, of course, constructed stone castles at home in Normandy before 1066. They were in touch with all the ideas about fortifications which were growing in Europe throughout the 11th and 12th centuries. Europe was now emerging triumphantly from the Dark Ages. The Viking raids were a thing of the past. There was a spirit of enquiry and hope in the air. Soon, the young powers of Europe would feel strong enough to embark on the great counter-offensive against Islam we call the Crusades. This change in Western Europe's political fortunes can be traced to the Feudal System - if so complex and variable theory of society can be called a system. But basically it meant that society as it emerged in the 11th century, was based upon personal service in return for ownership of land.

As the head of the pyramid was the King. In theory he was the fountain-head of power and honour. Under him were his great barons, both lay and ecclesiastical, who held their vast estates in return for clearly defined services, and for the men they could produce for the royal armies. The great barons, in their turn, had lesser barons underneath them, bound to them by the same obligation of personal loyalty and service that they owed to the king and so on down the line until we come to the peasantry, bound to the soil and the ultimate producers of the wealth and goods on which the whole pyramid was based. Even they in a very humble way had their own rights and a clearly defined place in society.

At what point in this pyramid did it become imperative for a man to build and own a castle? In Wales we can draw the line at the great Marcher barons and their immediate dependants. They, and the King, alone possessed enough power and wealth to build really important castles; although some of the lesser baronage might build minor strongholds in the more turbulent areas. The knights would live in their manors, where their houses could have a palisade for immediate security. The peasants, always the chief sufferers in mediaeval society, lived in their poor huts, clustered as near the castle or manor house as possible for safety, especially if they were on land newly conquered from the Welsh. There is a striking contrast between the villages in the high country, which remained in the hands of the Welsh, and those in the lower country where the Normans first extended their rule. In the Vale of Glamorgan, in South Gower and South Pembrokeshire, you still find a strong nucleus of houses grouped around the church or manor house. In the Welsh-speaking areas the pattern of settlement is much more open and scattered.

Around the great castles such as Chepstow, Pembroke and Cardiff, small townships grew up, sometimes encouraged by a charter from the Lord. Most of the towns of pre-industrial Wales began in this way. The castle was the centre of administration, the store-house of arms, the seat of justice and the symbol of power over the whole region it dominated. In it, at this period, lived the great man of the area.

This is what makes the medieval castle so radically different from the fortifications that had preceeded it in Britain. The Iron Age forts were tribal strongholds. The Roman forts were part of a vast state-owned system of public safety and defence. But the castle was the private possession of an individual feudal landlord, from which he exercised his feudal rights. When he started to convert his "motte and bailey" into something more substantial, his first thought would be to make certain that he had a final refuge, where his closest retainers, his family, his treasure and his records would be reasonably safe. Hence the rise in favour of that characteristic Norman construction the Keep, the strong central tower built on the most impregnable part of the castle site.

The term "Keep" is comparatively recent and did not come into use until the 16th century, by which time the mediaeval terms for castle construction were falling into oblivion. The Normans called this powerful last line of defence the Donjon. The idea had already been developed in France, where some splendid early examples can be seen at places like Loches. Equally impressive keeps or donjons were constructed in England in the years that followed the Conquest. There are fine early ones at Rochester and Porchester, while later on there came the most famous of them all, the White Tower of London. The general pattern of these keeps was that of a square tower with immensely thick walls. The lower floors and basement would be occupied by stores, with a draw well in the lowest of all. Here, too, might be the prison cells. By a strange irony the French word Donjon, which applied to the whole building, came to be transferred in English to the lowest of the rooms of the keep - now called dungeons.

The entrance, reached by a wooden ramp, would be on the first floor, whence a flight of internal steps led to the Great Hall. Here the Lord could feast and dispense justice, and his guard could sleep around the fire at night. On the floor above would be the private apartments, with a small chapel and a muniment room attached. The upper floor would contain the weapons needed for a successful defence, as the garrison hurled down stones or shot arrows from the roof above. The first of these great donjons to be built in Wales is that of Chepstow. This was constructed by William Fitzosbern time between 1067 and 1070: and although it has been added to at a later period, the bottom two stories can still give you the feeling of vast strength in the thick walls.

The keep thus replaced the motte in the newly strengthened castles. In some cases the new keep was even erected on top of the motte, as at Cardiff where an almost circular ring of walls is perched on the summit of the mound. These shell keeps, however, are not common.

The re-builder now turned his attention to the bailey. Here the dykes and wooden palisades would be replaced by stone walls and a gatehouse. The whole affair would present a far more serious defensive "enceinte" than the old style bailey, and this was just as well. For when we come to the 12th and the beginning of the 13th century we find that the Welsh were no longer totally outclassed in military technique. They had begun to learn from the invaders. They had become capable of making serious and damaging attacks on the new castles. The castle builders had to keep abreast of the times.

The history of warfare shows a constant see-saw between attack and defence. In our own time we saw how the machine gun killed the mass manoeuvering of armies in the First World War, and made battle a grim murderous slogging match. Then the tank appeared on the scene, that could crush the machine gun nests; with the result that the opening stages of the Second World War were brilliantly mobile. Before this ended, however, there were signs that the anti-tank weapons were going seriously to limit the tank's swift offensive power. So with the great square Keep and its attendant Bailey.

When the attacker had mastered the use of the battering ram and could even undermine the walls, something had to be done to keep the castle in business. Especially as the political scene in Wales changed once again as the Norman period came to an end.

On December 1st, 1142, Henry I died from his celebrated surfeit of lampreys. The whole of Wales breathed a sigh of relief and immediately proceeded to profit by the period of anarchy that followed. Once again, as so often in Welsh history, England's difficulty was Wales' opportunity. The succession was disputed between the Empress Matilda and Stephen. In England the royal grip on castle building weakened. Under the strong Norman kings every baron had to have royal permission, or, as it was known later on, a "licence to crenellate", before he could build a castle. The land now swarmed with these un-licensed castles, known by the name which has delighted all schoolboys for generations - "adulterine". For the Marcher barons in Wales it was not so much a question of building new "adulterine" castles but of hanging on to those they had already got.

Robert of Gloucester, the greatest of the Marcher lords, backed Matilda. The Welsh gleefully backed themselves. In the North, Owen Gwynedd swept to the gates of Chester. In the South, Welsh princes once again ruled in Cardigan and in the fertile lands around the valley of the Towy. As usual the Norman grip on the country of Dyfed (modern Pembrokeshire) and on Glamorgan and Gwent was far too strong to be shaken. But the Welsh had got back confidence in the future and that confidence grew all through the late 12th and most of the 13th century.

With the death of Stephen in 1154 the dynasty founded by William the Conqueror comes to an end. The Plantagenets take the stage in the person of the energetic, purposeful, restless and attractive Henry II. All through his busy life he had a great deal to do with Welsh affairs. It was in his reign and those of his successors, John and Richard I, that Welsh castle building took the next step forward. Most of the castles we loosely call Norman are more accurately Plantagenet in date. Even some of the square keeps, apart from that at Chepstow, were constructed in this period. Goodrich Castle, just over the border on the Wye in Herefordshire, has a fine square keep but it dates from the middle of the 12th century. The extensively remodelled keep at Coity may be earlier.

In fact, Wales cannot show many examples of the square keep. The Norman Conquest took far longer to make progress in the Principality, and it probably took the Welsh an equally long time to learn how to counter effectively the castle-building techniques of the invader. The motte and bailey type of structure, or some more elaborate variant of it, would remain viable for a considerable period in the border lands. The great age of keep-building starts in Wales - and indeed in England - during the reign of Henry II, and it only got into its stride a little later, when the square keep was going out of fashion.

For whatever their date, the owners were finding out that these imposing square keeps had their drawbacks. The corners were "dead ground" which couldn't be reached by flanking fire. They were thus vulnerable to attack by battering rams or by the miner's pick. Life inside the Donjon could not have been very comfortable even in the days of peace. These great towers were cold and draughty slabs, where people had to live crammed on top of one another.

The cooking arrangements were primitive, and the latrines functioned on what used to be known, euphemistically, in the Middle East as "the long drop" system. Our ancestors were used to doing without the creature comforts we now take for granted. When the Donjon was besieged the general stench must eventually have become intolerable. Of course the keep could be garrisoned by comparatively few defenders, but sooner or later an army would have to march to their relief. Clearly the castle had to become a more dynamic construction. The comparatively passive keep had no real future. Under the Plantagenets we see a stream of new influences and new ideas changing the concept of the castle in Wales.

3

The Power of Stone

The hundred odd years that stretch roughly from the death of King Stephen in 1154 to the Treaty of Montgomery in 1267, in the reign of Henry III, were decisive in the history of Wales. They saw the full flood of the Welsh revival. A new confidence seemed to suffuse the leaders of Wales. They had shown that the Normans were not invincible. They, too, could have their following of armed knights. They, too, could attack the Norman fortifications with success. They might even begin to build castles of their own! Furthermore, they had managed, in the face of common danger, to forget to some extent their chronic liability to internal feuds. Strong Welsh princes rose in the land. In the North, Owain Gwynedd, after a long and uniformly successful career, had united the fertile island of Anglesey with the mountain fastness of Snowdonia to make them the hard impregnable core of the principality of Gwynedd that extended almost to the walls of Chester. Powys, in mid-Wales, was not quite so lucky in its rulers, but at least did not lose territory on the English side of the border. In South Wales, Rhys ap Gruffydd, known to history by the simple but impressive title of the Lord Rhys, recreated the old kingdom of Deheubarth. He ejected the Norman lordships from the fertile valleys of the Teifi and the Towy. King Henry II, himself, called him his ally. He held his court in his castle of Dynefor just outside the modern town of Llandeilo, and his

power penetrated into every part of South Wales. Only the
coastal plain and the valleys of the Usk and Wye were independent of his will. Small wonder that the Marcher Lords
had to look to their defences. From this point we can date the
beginning of stone construction in so many of the Welsh
castles. Above all in those of South Wales.

Here lay the most sensitive area of confrontation. Here the
Lords Marcher had the most to lose, and here they made their
greatest effort to renew and fortify their castles according to
the most modern principles. Before we describe how they did
it, we should take a brief look at the two worlds that now
dramatically faced each other - the world of the Lords
Marcher and the world of the native Welsh.

The great Marcher families had now been established in
Wales, and especially in South Wales, for over fifty years.
During that period some of them had naturally inter-
married, or waxed or waned in power according to their abil-
ities and energy. But the estates they owned and held with all
the Marcher privileges were now firmly set. We meet the
names that constantly re-occur, not only in Welsh but in
English history as well, for the strength of their position in
Wales enabled the Marcher Lords to play decisive roles on a
bigger stage than than of the March.

Mortimers were firmly based in Radnorshire. There were
Bohuns just further south, Fitzalans and Corbets on the
Shropshire border and the de Breos family strongly placed in
the upper valleys of the Usk and Wye. Above all there was the
great house of Clare, with southern Monmouthshire, Glamorgan and eventually southern Pembrokeshire under its
control. We talk here of families being based in Pembrokeshire or Radnorshire, but we do this for convenience in order
to help a reader unfamiliar with the rich complexities of
Welsh territorial designations, to spot the scene of action on
a modern map. The shire system was not, in fact, extended to
Wales until after Edward I's Welsh Wars, and only completed after Henry VIII's Acts of Union. This was a long way
in the future. In the 12th and 13th centuries men still talked,

for example, of Cantref Mawr when they thought of the land on the north bank of the Towy valley, or of Gwent Uwch-coed for the country around Abergavenny and Gwent Iscoed for the lower reaches of the Usk and Wye

The Lords Marcher were remarkable men by any standard. There was the great Earl Richard of Clare, the famous "Strongbow", who answered King Dermot of Leinster's appeal for help in 1167 and crossed into Ireland from Milford Haven as the leader of what turned out to be almost a second version of the Norman Conquest. A gold rush of Flemings and Pembrokeshire knights followed him to carve out new estates in Southern Ireland, in the style to which they were already accustomed in South Wales. De Clare's strong castle of Pembroke gave him an excellent spring-board for his operation. So successful was he that he practically had the crown of Leinster in his grasp, until Henry II came hurrying down to control his over-proud vassal.

At the other end of the scale we can put William de Breos, who was a strange combination of daring warrior, pious churchman and ruthless enemy. He achieved a pre-eminence in infamy by a deed which shocked even the rough and tough men of the March, who were used to bloodshed. In 1175 he inherited the great lordship of Brecon and Upper Gwent. He invited Seisyll, the leading Welsh prince of the area, together with the most prominent Welshmen of Upper Gwent to his castle at Abergavenny for a friendly meeting. He and his followers suddenly fell upon the unsuspecting guests and massacred the lot. Worse still, he sent his retainers racing into Seisyll's country before the news of the treachery could spread. His armed thugs seized Seisyll's wife and then killed her seven year old son, Cadwaladr, as he lay in her arms. This was barbarity of a high order. Yet the same William de Breos would never pass a wayside cross or shrine without stopping to pray, and spoke to children in the street in order to hear them murmer "God bless you" in answer to his greeting.

Not all the boldness and ruthless initiative lay on the Marcher side. Welshmen could be equally daring. In 1158 a dramatic incident occurred which became one of the great legendary exploits of the Border, and it took place in the heart of territory which had long been regarded as a completely Norman stronghold. In the hills of Glamorgan, at Senghenydd, lived Ivor ap Meurig who was short in stature and was therefore called Ivor Bach (little Ivor) by the Welsh. He was however great in courage and daring. He had a territorial grievance against his overlord Earl William, the ruler of Glamorgan. Ivor resolved to do the impossible and kidnap the Earl in his own castle of Cardiff. This must have seemed a mad escapade, for not only was the castle strongly guarded by the Earl's men at arms, but he had a strong body of archers in the little township now established around the castle. Ivor however succeeded in climbing up the huge motte which still exists in the centre of the castle grounds. He scaled the wall and got into the Earl's apartment, seized him and his wife Hawise together with his young son Robert, and whisked the family away to the hills before the alarm could be raised. He got all the concessions he asked for before he released the Earl.

Such was life in the Marches of Wales - rough, constantly dangerous, but still full of colour and even stimulating to men of imagination. The clash between the Anglo-Normans and the Welsh was not simply a tale of bloodshed and burning. The two races learnt from each other and even learnt to respect each other. It is more than likely that the Celtic stories of Arthur were transmitted to the Anglo-Norman barons through the medium of the "latimers", or interpreters, in the castles of South Wales, and so passed into European literature. Geoffrey of Monmouth, whatever may be thought of the truth of his history, was a man of the Marches and a great writer in addition. But the most attractive of all the literary figures on the Marches of South Wales was Gerald de Barri, or Geraldus Cambrensis (Gerald the Welshman). He came of that mixed Norman-Welsh stock that made such a notable contribution to the affairs in Wales in mediaeval times, being the grandson of the famous Nest, "the Helen of Wales". He, himself, was born in the castle of

Manorbier in South Pembrokeshire, and one of his earliest memories was of being hurried to safety as a child of five, as the Welsh threatened the castle. He grew up to be an ecclesiastic of restless talent and ambition, proud of his Welsh-Norman descent, and with his heart set on making the see of St. David's into an independent archbishopric. He was a scholar educated in Paris, and had a marvellously sprightly pen. We know him intimately as we know few figures of the Middle Ages, when men were not given to self revelation in prose. He toured Wales with Archbishop Baldwin in 1188 to preach the Third Crusade, and out of that journey came our most vivid picture of Wales and the March as the 12th century drew to its close. Gerald is the source of most of the thrilling, entertaining and at times unbelievable stories that have been the joy of historians ever since. To him we must turn to see the manner of life on the Welsh side. Gerald paints an attractive picture. The Welsh in the hills were largely dependent for their wealth on the herds of cattle. Houses were flimsy affairs built of woven osiers and easily repaired or replaced. The Welsh existed on a somewhat spartan diet. Meat, cheese, milk, oats and butter were the principal foods, since the land was not geared for extensive agriculture in the style of the feudal manors of England. Hospitality was a duty. Guests were entertained with music, harping and story telling. The Lord lived in his "llys" or court. In the great hall built of wood he was guarded by his "teulu", his family of retainers pledged to support him to the death. Personal loyalty was highly prized, and every Welshman took a profound interest in his descent, a trait that has survived to this day.

The Welsh could be treacherous to outsiders and could give way to sudden panic in battle. But they soon recovered. They were a high-spirited proud race who, says Gerald, "deem it ignoble to die in their beds and an honour to fall on the field of battle". Their lightly armoured troops might not be able to stand up to heavily armoured knights in open warfare, but their nimbleness made them formidable in ambushes in close country, and in the guerrilla warfare that was their natural form of attack. They regarded themselves as

CONWAY. Planned in two halves: To the left, the Royal apartments, to the right, the garrison's headquarters.

nobody's inferior. Gerald relates for us the story which breathes the whole spirit of the Welsh national revival.

Henry II was marching through South Wales on a punitive expedition, when he met an old Welshman at Pencader. He asked the veteran how long the Welsh could resist. The old man replied with the memorable words "This nation, O King, may now as in former times be harrassed, and in a great measure weakened and destroyed by your and other powers, and it will often prevail by its laudable exertions: but it can never be totally subdued through the wrath of man, unless the wrath of God shall concur. Nor do I think that any other nation than this of Wales, or any other language, whatever may hereafter come to pass, shall on the day of severe examination before the Supreme Judge answer for this corner of the earth". Today these words are inscribed on slate on the modern memorial at the side of the road in Pencader, and they still speak Welsh there!

With this sort of spirit animating their enemies the Lords Marcher in South Wales were more than ready to reconstruct their castles. Princes like the Lord Rhys had forced them to relinquish their more isolated strongholds far inland, but they clung like limpets to the sites nearer the coast, and those guarding the coastal plain. Along this plain ran the great road to the West which had acquired a new importance with the Anglo-Norman settlement in Ireland. A roll call of impressive castles lies along it, most them placed on the lowest river crossings so that they could be easily revictualled from the sea. Wherever possible the Welsh were to be firmly pinned into their hills. If you follow the modern road to the West you will find most of the castle ruins along or within easy reach of it.

Chepstow was the first of them, guarding the passage of the Wye. Then comes Newport at the mouth of the Usk, and Cardiff guarding the Taff. The road went inland to cut across the Vale of Glamorgan, with the powerful strongholds of Coity and the new castle at Bridgend watching the Blaenau, or the hill county of Glamorgan. You never knew when another Ivor Bach might issue from its wooded fast-

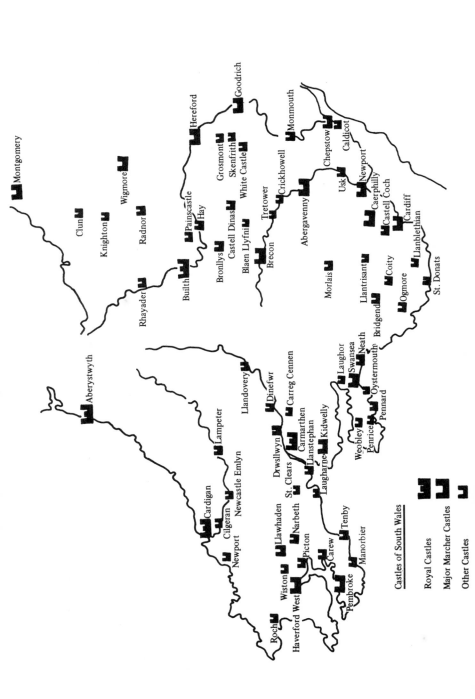

Castles of South Wales

Royal Castles

Major Marcher Castles

Other Castles

Montgomery
Clun
Knighton
Wigmore
Radnor
Rhayader
Builth
Painscastle
Hay
Bronllys
Castell Dinas
Blaen Llyfni
Brecon
Hereford
Grosmont
Skenfrith
White Castle
Tretower
Crickhowell
Abergavenny
Monmouth
Goodrich
Chepstow
Caldicot
Usk
Newport
Caerphilly
Castell Coch
Cardiff
Llanblethian
St. Donats
Morlais
Llantrisant
Coity
Ogmore
Bridgend
Neath
Swansea
Laughor
Oystermouth
Pennard
Penrice
Weobley
Kidwelly
Llanstephan
Laugharne
Carmarthen
Carreg Cennen
Dinefwr
Llandovery
Llanelly
Aberystwyth
Lampeter
Newcastle Emlyn
Cardigan
Cilgeran
Newport
Drwsllwyn
St. Clears
Narbeth
Llawhaden
Picton
Wiston
Haverford West
Roch
Carew
Tenby
Manorbier
Pembroke

nesses! Next came Neath and Swansea, both guarding river crossings that could be reinforced from the sea. The same reason led to the strengthening of Lougher (Llwchwr), Kidwelly (Cydweli) and Llanstephan at the mouth of the Towy. Carmarthen on the lowest crossing of that river deserves special mention since it was always a royal castle. The King too, could claim to be one of the Marcher Lords!

Beyond Carmarthen came Laugharne (Talacharn), St. Clear's on the Taff, Narberth, Llawhaden, and so, via Carew to the great fortress of Pembroke, the key to Ireland. Naturally there were also strong castles to guard the old Fleming settlements high up Milford Haven, grouped around Haverfordwest with outliers further north still at Newport (Pembs). The King, somewhat later, even got a foothold back in Cardigan.

A second group of castles lay on the Eastern borderland in modern Monmouthshire, Breconshire, Radnorshire. The Welsh still occupied the hill ground, while the Normans had pushed far up the fertile valleys of the Usk, the Wye and the Severn. In the northern end of this section of the March the great castle of Montgomery was, as it were, the power house of all Norman strength in the borderland. Further south came strongholds like Clun, Wigmore and Radnor, with - away to the East–the castle of Ludlow. A string of castles held the Wye and the upper valley of the Usk. Painscastle, in the hills of Radnorshire, still shows a great maze of earthworks originally planned as a giant "motte and bailey" at the end of the 12th Century but heavily reconstructed later. Further up the Wye, and a constant source of irritation to the Welsh, was Builth, but a line of strongholds led to the equally exposed castle of Brecon. These were Clifford, Hay, Pipton and Bronllys. In northern Monmouthshire, Abergavenny, the scene of the de Breos massacre, was the principle stronghold, with Crickhowell and Tretower linking it with the upper Usk.

Fronting the Black Mountains was the interesting group of castles known as the "tri-lateral" or "the three castles" - White Castle, Grosmont and Skenfrith. They always went together. Whoever held one held the others. They had a series of owners, including a de Breos session, for half the Marches sooner or later passed through the hands of that restless family. Then came Herbert de Burgh, who reconstructed most of them, and from time to time the King. Behind this triangle of defence lay Monmouth on the Wye. Further down on the Usk was the castle of Usk, and a few miles to the east, Raglan. Raglan's glory and splendour, however, belong to a far later date. Always on guard at the mouth of the Wye was the oldest and most elaborate of them all - Chepstow.

These names form an impressive list, but in addition to these two great groups of castles we must also remember the numerous smaller strongholds, especially in Monmouthshire and Glamorgan that, as it were, clustered in their shade. There is hardly a town or village in the Eastern Marches or along the coastal plain which does not have traces of some sort of fortification near at hand, and most of them were first turned into stone or elaborated and reconstructed in the period which we are discussing. But when we come to select an example of a castle that will show us exactly what the new type of fortress of the late 12th and early 13th century looked like, we are in a difficulty. Castles were living things. If they were correctly placed to begin with on a strong defensive site, as at Chepstow, Pembroke or Carmarthen, there was no point in building a new centre elsewhere. The existing site would have to be used. The walls, the towers, the keep and even the motte and bailey would be altered, added to, or incorporated in each successive improvement.

It is tempting to construct a logical theory of castle development with each new stage tidily and inevitably growing out of the previous one. Thus in theory, we ought to be able to say that the motte clearly changed into the keep, that stone-built curtain walls replaced the wooden palisades of the bailey, and that the first type of keep would naturally be a shell keep planted on the summit of the existing motte and again replacing a wooden palisade. Then we could logically point out that the square stone keep would replace the shell keep as offering a great step forward in safety, a stronger construction altogether than the flimsier shell keep, perched on a mount of earth that could easily be undermined. The square keep in its turn would be replaced by the round keep with no blind ground on the awkward corners.

In the meantime the simple stone curtain wall, that had replaced the wooden palisade of the first bailey, would also be elaborated by towers designed to allow the defenders to see along the wall and prevent any attempt to get near it. If the site allowed it, a second bailey might be added to the first, presenting the attackers with a sort of a steeple chase over stone fences before they reached the final core of the defence, the keep. Even this complexity might have left one outstanding weakness in the defensive strength of this new type of castle - the gate. The entrance to a castle was always a danger point. There were well established techniques for bursting into a weak gatehouse, from the simple trick of firing a wooden doorway with cartloads of blazing hay to powerful battering rams. We shall therefore see the gatehouse growing in complexity, strength and cunning until it displaces the keep as the real power centre of the castle. All is now set for the appearance on the scene, at the end of the period we are considering, of that final masterpiece of the fortress builder's art in the Middle Ages, the almost impregnable stronghold of the Concentric Castle. Only the advent of gunpowder was going to shake these brilliantly planned concentric walls and towers.

This is a clear-cut account of how castle building might have developed over two hundred years - each new trick of attack countered by a new trick of defence, the old methods immediately discarded for the new as they entered Wales from England and the Continent. There is no doubt that this logical pattern makes sense. Such changes did occur. The castle at the end of these two centuries was a radically different affair from the simple motte and bailey. But, of course, new developments didn't occur in a carefully arranged sequence in each individual castle. Indeed modern scholarship has thrown doubts on the theory that the motte and bailey inevitably developed into the stone-built castle. It could be regarded as a purely military device adapted to temporary conditions. Fashions overlapped. There is no proof that Shell Keeps always preceded the Square Keep: both could be favoured at the same time. Architects and castle owners could be conservative in their tastes. The great lord might insist on having a square keep when his architect would have preferred a round one; for the men who built these castles must have had the same experience as anyone who has decided to build his own house today—nothing ever really turned out as originally planned! And all building involves a mental and social battle between the builder and the man who pays.

We know the names of a great many of the men who paid for these new castles: and if they were lesser men they didn't always do it with their own money. William de Camville, who had to re-build Llanstephan around 1192 after it had been destroyed by the Lord Rhys, had to borrow the cash from the Sheriff of Gloucester! But we have very few records of the sums of money involved since most of these castles were built by the Lords Marcher and their followers. In the continual exchange of estates, civil wars, sudden death and intermarriage of families in the Marches of Wales, records had small chance of survival. It was a different matter when castles were held by the King. The administrative machinery of government centre around the royal court and good administration depends on the keeping of records, especially when it comes the the question of dues to be paid and taxes to be collected. After all, William the Conqueror had set the example in that great combined census and tax we call Doomsday Book. Later on, the records of the royal courts and the Exchequer were carefully kept, although in an astonishingly inconvenient manner. Chancery records for example were written on parchment, and filed by the the incredible metod of sewing together in sequence all the skins of parchment used in a given year. If you wanted to examine a document you had to unroll the whole collection, and a year could produce a string of records yards long. Maybe this strange arrangement was devised for ease of transport in the days when the whole administrative machinery had to follow the King in his travels, but it had its grave inconveniences. When Richard I defeated King Philip Augustus of France in 1194 he collected the whole of the French archives as well.

Henry II was a particularly restless King, always on the move. His administrators complained that they never knew on one day where he would be on the next and it is tempting to think that some of the Exchequer accounts, known as the Great Roll of the Pipe, must have been carted after him by harrassed officials, and unrolled in damp castles in Wales to settle some obscure point. Later, all rolls and documents were kept in the Tower or Westminster Palace. It is from the Great Rolls of the Pipe of Henry's day that we find that £128.16s. was spent on work at Llantilio (White Castle) between 1184 and 1186. In modern money this would amount to many thousands of pounds and would cover the cost of the curtain wall. This sum gives us a yardstick to judge the costs in other places. Thus, when we find that £43.17s.7d. was spent in 1186 at the nearby castle of Skenfrith, we can be certain that it went to the cost of repairing and strengthening the existing wooden defences and not in replacing them with stone.

This money would be paid to a building team working under a master builder, who in the Middle Ages would combine all the functions of the modern architect, contractor and superintendent of works. Again we are ignorant of the names of the men who worked on even the most impressive of the South Wales castles. It would be pleasant to know who created such military masterpieces as the South East Tower of Goodrich with its powerful stone spurs, the Gatehouse of Kidwelly or the vast round Keep of Pembroke. Later on, when we come to look at the ring of castles built by Edward I in North Wales, we will have reasonably full royal records on which to rely. We will be able to salute the architect by name - Master James of St. George, and we even know the appropriate level of his level of salary - around£6,000 a year in modern money. The unknown architects of the South Wales castles may not have earned that sort of money, but they must have been considerable men nevertheless. And like all the mediaeval builders, they were not afraid to travel. The elite of the profession were the cathedral builders and we know that men like Villard de Honnecourt, the Picard master whose book of architectural drawings has survived to delight us today, travelled extensively through Northern Europe, Austria and Hungary. The master builder, Eudes de Montreul, actually went with St. Louis on his Crusade, and Master James of St. George himself may well have been to the Holy Land or seen the walls of Byzantium.

These travelling masters would be wide open to any new idea or technique. I picture them a little like the bold engineers of the 19th century, who were willing to journey to the most remote territories of the old British Empire to fling railway bridges over gorges in the Himalayas, blast roads through the passes of the North West Frontier or construct vast barrages across the Nile. The Marches of South and mid Wales were certainly wild and remote. To some of the newly arrived craftsmen, working for instance on a place like Carreg Cennen, perched on a high limestone crag facing the wilderness of the Black Mountain in Carmarthenshire, it must have seemed as if they had been sent to the North West Frontier of mediaeval Europe.

The tools of castle construction would be the same as those used on the Cathedrals, including big cranes for hoisting, worked either by a capstan or a tread-mill. There would be elaborate scaffolding, ladders and wheelbarrows and a nucleus of a team of trained men for the skilled work like stone cutting. In the later castles we find ashlar construction - stones of regular shape and size laid in level courses. This demanded skilled craftsmen. Supporting them would be a big body of unskilled workmen, probably drawn from the immediate neighbourhood and ordered to work on the castle. Sometimes a special quarry would be opened near the site. Wales was lucky in this - good building stone was usually found close to the scene of operations. There was no need to import stone, as in the chalk country of Southern England, where stone from Caen in Normandy was ferried across the channel or commissioned from the distant quarries of Maidstone, Barnack or Quarr. Wood would also be relatively easy to get. Wales was densely forested in places in these early days. Lead might have to come from further afield, even from Derbyshire.

But whether the material came from near or far, building a castle of stone according to the new ideas was a considerable organisational feat, especially as several of these new castles might be under construction at the same time. The royal records generally show intense activity in the first few years, when a large proportion of the money was spent. Clearly if you were building a castle in the Marches of South Wales you were usually doing it so to annoy or defy your Welsh neighbour. He, in turn, would try his utmost to wreck your work, so the builders worked might and main to get the circuit of the walls built up to some sort of defensive height in the first year. There are records of building continuing through the winter - an extremely rare procedure in the Middle Ages when construction work usually stopped as the cold weather approached. The unfinished walls were then thatched over to protect them from frost. The completed walls would be coated with plaster or whitewash to act as a stone preservative. At White Castle, in Northern Monmouthshire, you can still see traces of this plaster on some of the walls. No doubt it was from this white coating that the castle got its later name. In its early career it was simply referred to as Llantilio. A newly built castle like White Castle must have looked far different from the grey broken ruins we see there today. We must picture the castles of South Wales glittering in whitewash, with high pitched roofs, banners flying from the battlements on great occasions, the courtyards alive with the coming and going of the garrison and their horses. For after all, the horse was an extremely important factor in feudal life. The man on horseback was the man of power. A castle could not be a real castle if it did not contain ample room for the stables.

Those new-built castles must have been a source of pride to their owners. You can sense that pride in the names they gave to their creations. Richard the Lion Heart called his great new castle overlooking the Seine in Normandy his Chateau Gaillard - his "saucy castle", which alas! did not prevent it falling into the hands of his enemy, Philip Augustus, King of France, after an epic siege. Some of this pride must have come from the feeling that the new castle was abreast and even ahead of the times. We can classify these improvements under three headings - the keep, the curtain walls and the gatehouse. We have already seen that the concept of the square keep as the last defensive line, the ultimate strong-hold,was an essential part of the design of the earlier Norman Castles in stone. But we have already noted that from the defence point of view, the square keep had a great weakness at the corners. One of the earliest improvements in Wales was the substitution of a round for a square keep. There are numerous and impressive examples scattered over the Southern march. The origin of the round keep, like so many of the changes in castle design, is still uncertain. It has been suggested that it had forerunners in the buttressed round keeps of Eigenburg and Reichenburg in Germany and that German influence came to British castle builders as a result of the captivity and ransom of Richard I. France, too, can show round keeps of an early period. Whereever the idea came from, the Welsh castle builders took it up with enthusiasm. They appreciated that besides presenting no vulnerable corners or dead ground, a round tower is more economical in space than a square one, and allows for stone vaulting and a dome of stone on top. The danger of fire is thus severely limited.

We can take the great round keep of Pembroke - one of the finest in Britain - as an example. It is also one of the earliest in Wales and was probably built by the famous William Marshall, who had the distinction of being one of the few self made men in that hereditary-conscious age, and who was rewarded by Richard I with the hand of Isabella, the heiress to the vast estates of the De Clares. This made him a great man not only in the Marches of Wales but in England and Europe as well. His keep - if we may safely assume he ordered it to be built-stood over 100ft. high when complete. It had five stories, connected by a winding interior staircase inset in the 16 ft. deep wall. The entrance was on the first floor. The second floor had a two-light lancet window. The fifth floor was a sort of fighting top, backed by a stone dome. The holes are still visible into which fitted the beams supporting a wooden gallery around the top storey. From the gallery the defenders could rain down stones and other offensive weapons on anyone approaching the foot of the tower. The lowest storey had a sloping plinth - any stone dropped from above would ricochet out among the attackers. William Marshall may have been the "trend setter" in round donjons or keeps. We find strong ones at Tretower and Bronllys and again at Skenfrith, where it is set almost in the middle of the castle enclosure.

We can describe these castles as "enceinte" castles - an enceinte being simply the bailey, that is the area enclosed by high walls. The great donjon, the last resort of the defenders, could be set in the middle of it or else placed at the strongest point. We look next at the walls which enclosed the "enceinte", or as we must call them technically "the curtain".

The simplest curtain would be a ring of plain high walls encircling the area to be defended. This simple form might have been the first curtain constructed at White Castle.

Ogmore, near the sea in Glamorgan, is particularly interesting. This castle was reconstructed in stone in the early 13th century, but the south side of the inner ward was still left as an earthen bank.

It was not long before castle builders realised the serious defects of a simple wall, however thick. Attackers could get near it undetected, to set up battering rams under wooden sheds, or else begin mining. In answer to these dangers, towers were set up at regular intervals - and round towers for preference. The defenders could look along the wall from the

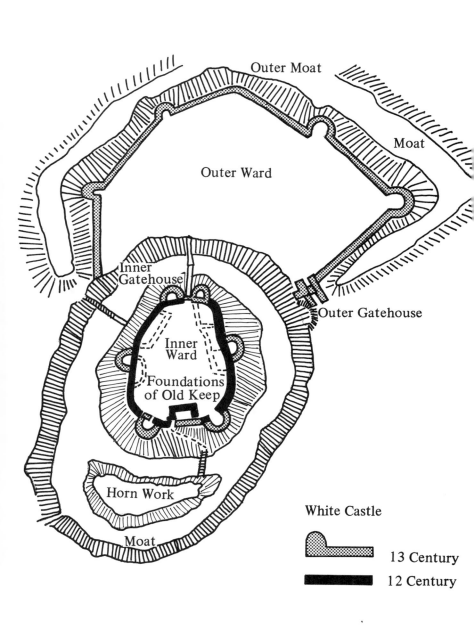

Outer Moat

Moat

Outer Ward

Inner Gatehouse

Outer Gatehouse

Inner Ward

Foundations of Old Keep

Horn Work

Moat

White Castle

13 Century

12 Century

safety of these projecting towers and shoot down anyone who approached it. The defenders would also need to drop stones, and anything else unpleasant they could lay their hands on, directly upon the attackers from the top of the wall. To enable them to do this, hoardings, or bretaches (brattices), were set up to jut out and overlook the base of the curtain wall. In many castles a row of holes can be seen running high along the curtain. These are the putlog holes, from the putlogs or great beams supporting the hoarding. These overlooking hoardings could be permanent, or installed when danger threatened.

A further development of the hoarding idea came when, at certain points of the castle enceinte, especially on the tops of the towers and the gatehouse, overhanging galleries were constructed of stone, with openings for discharging missiles. These are known as "Machicolations". The gate house of Kidwelly is well provided with them, and they reach splendid proportions on the towers of Raglan. At Rhuddlan, there were even "box machicolations" - small, narrow turrets which jutted out of parts of the curtain wall and gave added protection to long stretches of it between the towers.

Beside the outflanking towers and the overlooking hoardings, the curtain wall needed a few other features to make it serviceable. Along the top of the wall ran the "allure", or parapet walk. The soldiers on the allure were protected on the enemy side by the battlements. The battlements in turn were divided at regular intervals, the solid section being known as the "merlon" and the open section as the "crenel". From crenel came the word to "crenellate", and "a licence to crenellate", that is to make gaps in the parapet wall and so make a tower or curtain ready for defence, could usually be granted only by the King. Sometimes these gaps were fitted with shutters hanging on swivels anchored on the merlons on either side. These shutters gave the archers extra protection when firing, just as the merlons allowed them to load in safety. You can see the grooves for the shutters in Caernarfon Castle, while at Cardiff the Marquis of Bute, in his Victorian restoration, refitted a part of the wall with shutters. They may not be original, but they give an excellent idea of how merlons, crenels and shutters fitted together in the Middle Ages.

So the keep was improved, and the curtain wall strengthened with towers and hoardings. The bailey might even be divided into two to give an extra obstacle if the attackers forced the curtain wall. One source of possible weakness remained - the gate. It was no good building defiant walls if the attackers found it easy to rush in and break down the entrance to the enceinte. Military engineers had early recognised the danger and continually developed the difficulties of gaining entrance. The actual portal was now set deep between high flanking towers, well provided with arrow slits. Over it would be a strong arch on which would be an elaborate guard room. Here was the windlass which cranked up the portcullis, a grating shod with iron points. Once the portcullis was down it was impossible to open the outer doors. Above the passage which led under the guard room were a series of holes, - the grimly named "murder" holes - through which the defenders in the guard room could shower down missiles on any attacker brave enough to have penetrated so far. In a big gatehouse there could be a second portcullis at the end of the passage leading out into the ward. In Caernarfon there are actually three in the main entrance of the King's Gate.

The gatehouse had to embody one more important structure - the drawbridge. Most castles were surrounded by a moat, the "fosse". Where streams could be dammed the moat would be water-filled, as at White Castle. At Caerphilly there is a whole series of moats, on such a splendid scale that they look like miniature lakes. Over such big wet moats the gateway would be approached on a long tressle bridge - with the last section acting as the drawbridge. Where water was not available a deeply cut ditch in the rock wall could be equally effective. There are impressive rock ditches at Carreg Cennen and at Goodrich.

The drawbridge could be drawn up on chains and the beams on which the chains were fastened could themselves be retracted into slots set in the gatehouse wall and called "chases". But this was a cumbersome method. Later draw-bridges worked on the see-saw or balance principle, turning on a central pivot, so by shifting weight the whole bridge tipped up with the inner section dropping into a specially prepared pit inside the entrance. We call them drawbridges, but turning bridges would be more correct. The outer section lifted to close the entrance passage, thus adding to the ob-stacles blocking the entrance. No drawbridge or portcullis survives in Wales, although at the Queen's Gate of Caern-arfon you can see exactly what the arrangements were for the "tip-up" type of drawbridge; and in the gatehouses of castles like Kidwelly, Oystermouth and Llanstephan you can see the chases, the "murder holes" and the slot down which the portcullis descended.

Once again the third Marquis of Bute can come to our rescue. At Cardiff and at Castell Coch, some seven miles to the north, at the entrance of the Taff valley, his architect William Burges carefully reconstructed the portcullis and the drawbridge. At Castell Coch the drawbridge operated over a deep-cut rock ditch. The portcullis and the draw-bridge counterbalance each other and can be operated in a surprisingly short time by just two men.

The gatehouse builders were still not satisfied. They felt that it would be a great advantage if the first rush of the att-ackers could be met at a point beyond the main gateway and the moat. So to guard the approach across it, they built a Barbican. This was usually a defensive semi-circle with its back to the moat, but it could take a variety of forms. In Caer-philly the barbican is on a gigantic scale, almost a castle in itself. This can be contrasted with the tiny semicircle out-side Oystermouth where the barbican was probably a simple wooden pallisade. In between, the Marches of Wales can show barbicans of all shapes, sizes and construction. Good-rich has an unusually well preserved barbican, designed to force the attacker to capture two bridges set at right angles to each other before he reached the main gatehouse. This barbican even had a small gatehouse of its own, complete with drawbridge.

Carreg Cennen shows a similar complexity. The elaborate barbican contained a steep ramp, ending again in a right angled turn and a tower protecting the main drawbridge across the very deep, dry ditch. Unfortunately many Welsh barbicans have now disappeared. They were the first and most convenient quarry for building stones when the castles fell into decay.

Finally most castles possess what is called a "postern", a small gateway sometimes incorporated in the main gatehouse which could be easily blocked and would allow people to slip in and out without the garrison having to raise the drawbridge and portcullis. This could be particularly useful when the castle was under siege. So the gatehouse grew and developed in complexity until it became the strongest part or the castle and replaced the old donjon or keep. When White Castle was reconstructed in the middle of the 13th century the architects felt that the old donjon had become so uselesss compared with the gatehouse that they pulled it down altogether. In Kidwelly and later in Harlech the gatehouse dominates the scene. It was as if the leader of the defence was no longer thinking of a last ditch refuge but had come forward right to the front of the battle.

It is now time for us to go inside the castle to see the life that was lived within the new towers, curtain walls and gatehouses rising all over the Marches of South Wales.

HARLECH. The perfect defensive site. Only treachery or gunfire could capture it.

BEAUMARIS. A mathematically perfect concentric design.

4

Towards the Impregnable Castle

When the visitor goes through the gateway and into the outer bailey of most of the Welsh castles today, he may find it difficult to make out the meaning and purpose of most of the ruined walls and roofless halls he sees all around him. Unlike a Roman fort, a mediaeval castle had no standardized lay-out. It was irregular, adapting its structure to the physical advantages offered by the site and to the special purpose for which the castle was built. It usually contained certain buildings common to all castles and which were an essential part of the life of the powerful throughout the Middle Ages. The time had gone by when the whole of the living accommodation was confined to the donjon or keep.

The most important of the domestic buildings was the Hall. This was the centre of the social life of the castle. Here the lord or the castellian dined in state at his high table. Massive fireplaces were replacing the open hearths in the middle of the floor as the method of heating the great room. It would also be used as a court, for the castle in peacetime was the legal and administrative centre of the countryside around it. Halls varied in size,from the modest ones at Llanstephan and Carreg Cennen to the magnificent (and newly restored) hall at Caerphilly, which was almost regal in splendour, as befitted the great Marcher house of de Clare.

In Caerphilly the hall was at ground level, probably because of the very scale of its construction. But the hall could also be on the first floor, leaving space for storage underneath. In early plans the Lord's private rooms would lead directly out of the hall, perhaps by a special staircase. All through the 13th century these rooms were becoming more elaborate as the standard of living rose. They would include a great chamber in which the lord's family could meet their private guests, the solar or the lord's retiring rooms and the bower, the special domain of the ladies. That most important area, the kitchen, was usually set apart from these suites of living rooms. If the castle contained a big garrison, cooking had to be on a considerable scale with all the aromas and heat that this entailed. The kitchen would have impressive fireplaces and ample water supply. The diet supplied by the efforts of the cooks would strike us as monotonous - there were no deep-freeze arrangements to keep supplies fresh through the winter! They could also be salty or highly spiced. When you read some of the mediaeval cookery books which have survived it seems a marvel that our ancestors were not dead from indigestion by the time they were forty. But more of the dishes described in such manuals would be for great occasions. On ordinary days the diet of even a great lord would be far more modest.

Sanitary arrangements were not so primitive as popular fancy depicts them. Most of the principal apartments in a big castle like Goodrich had their garde-robes or privies. In Conway these could be emptied outside the castle walls in time of siege, since they were corbelled out under the battlements. In Chepstow, some of the privies were arranged to flush directly into the river Wye far below. Otherwise they were emptied by carrying away the buckets in the same style as the vast majority of lavatories were cleared, almost down to the beginning of the 20th century. Garde-robes or their equivalents were a feature of the royal palaces of Europe, at Versailles and Schoenbrunn in the enlightened 18th century. Besides, our ancestors were more accustomed to strong, natural smells than we who are born into the Age of the Deodorant.

One thing, however, would certainly have struck a

modern visitor if he had been transported back to a castle of the Middle Ages. It was a dark, if not a damp place to live in. Oil for lamps was expensive and inefficient. People tended to go to bed early in winter. The return of Spring brought a marvellously exhilarating release to the spirit and mind as well as to the body. You can sense this from the songs and the literature which have survived from the period. Again we need not picture every 12th and 13th century marcher baron as a crude tyrannical thug in armour, laying his iron hand on his serfs and in perpetual rebellion against his King. Gilbert de Clare had at one time in his service Geoffrey of Aspale whose commentaries on part of Aristotle's natural history have come down to us, Gerald the Welshman, Geoffrey of Monmouth and Walter Map were all the products of the Marches. Most castles, moreover, had one man who could make some claim to education, the Chaplain. In the Middle Ages, religion suffused the whole business of living and was not relegated to separate compartments of specialised experience. The Chapel was felt to be essential a part of the castle as the barbican or the gatehouse, and was suitably ornamented. A curious example of the combination of the practical and spiritual occurs at Chepstow where Martin's Tower had its own portcullis which, when lifted, fitted into the far end of the chapel. The chapel moreover was no rough affair but one of the most beautiful apartments of the castle.

A great lord, of course, did not spend all his time in one castle. He moved with his retinue around his estates. Certainly in the early days he moved because it was easier to go and eat the food where it was produced than to transport it for miles over indifferent tracks!

Later on, when matters became more settled, the great castle might be the official seat of a family, as at Goodrich which the Valences and, after them, the powerful Talbots made their principal residence. Or it might, like Caerphilly, be the chief centre of administration but not the place where the owner delighted to reside. Above all, the castle was a fighting machine; the ultimate justification for all the money and thought spent upon it came in time of war.

Mediaeval warfare was as much an affair of sieges as of pitched battles. It was always difficult to keep large mobile armies in the field. Supplying a vast army of knights, squires, archers, pikemen and their attendant retinue could tax national resources. A resolutely defended castle could tie up big forces of attackers with small numbers of defenders, and thus have a decisive influence on a campaign. The castle had many advantages on its side. The defenders were mostly under cover - the archers, for example, had plenty of time to use the cross-bow, the most powerful individual weapon available before the invention of gunpowder and one possessing great range and accuracy. It is on record that a Victorian enthusiast with a carefully reconstructed cross-bow succeeded in firing an arrow across the Menai Straits! But the cross-bow took time to crank up, and in the field it had a serious rival in the long-bow.

This, by the way, seemed to have originated in the Marches of South Wales in the land of Gwent, and South Welsh bowmen were later to play a great part in the history of the Hundred Years War. To this day the men of Llantrisant in the Vale of Glamorgan remember that their ancestors were known as the "Black Army" and helped to win the victories of Crecy and Poitiers. The long bow in the hands of an expert could be a real quick-fire weapon, and it could also possess great penetrative power. Geraldus Cambrensis relates the story of an archer who fired an arrow that not only penetrated the door of a South Wales castle but pinned an armoured knight behind it to the saddle of his horse. Maybe that was pulling the long bow with a vengeance! Long bow or cross bow - no matter! The defender behind his castle wall had the advantage.

The attacker, however, was not without resources. He had, first of all, to select a possible weak point on the curtain wall where he had a chance of opening a breach. He might try to do this by undermining the wall but this wasn't easy if the wall was defended by a moat. Wet moats could be drained, but the defence in White Castle and at Caerphilly had made special arrangements to protect points where drainage could be attempted. Besides, a great many Welsh castles stood on hard rock where mining was a hopeless affair from the start. No one would attempt it against Harlech, Pembroke or Carreg Cennen.

There remained the possibility of battering at a selected section of the wall with powerful stone-throwing engines - the artillery of the Middle Ages. Of these there were a variety, from giant slings called perrieres, to the catapults and mangonels that seemed to have been derived from the machinery of the Romans. Like all old soldiers, the army delighted in giving these monsters nicknames. At the siege of Acre in Palestine, Philip Augustus built a great catapult which was immediately christened Malvoisine, "the bad neighbour"! The Military Orders had one they called rather smugly, "God's own sling". We know the Welsh now possessed similar siege engines. They were used freely by the Lord Rhys and his sons against the castles of William de Breos, although their nicknames have not come down to us. These engines would be protected by temporary earthworks or palisades as they battered away at the curtain wall. They were not exactly accurate but they were extremely persistent. The garrison might try to destroy them by sorties or set them on fire. This was difficult, for the West did not possess the secret of the remarkably effective Byzantine combustible called Greek Fire. Again, the defence could not use mangonels or catapults to quite the same extent as the attack, since these machines needed space around them, and the walls and towers of a castle were certainly short on space. If the curtain had been severely shaken, attempts could be made to crack it open with the aid of the Cat, a huge battering ram protected from the missiles of the defenders by a stout shed.

By the middle of the 13th century a more formidable and accurate assault machine was coming into use - which remained the most powerful weapon in the attacker's armoury until the advent of the early cannons around 1325. This was the Trebuchet. The idea may have originated in China, where in 1004 we hear of a huge stone-thrower constructed out of a beam pivoted on a frame and powered by a team of soldiers pulling on ropes. In Europe the first record of a trebuchet seems to be at the Siege of Lisbon in 1147, when it was operated by a team of 100 men in relays. Then the man-team was replaced by a cassion of rocks at the short end of the pivoted beam. This cassion could be raised by a powerful pulley and the shot released by a trigger. The earlier types of stone-throwers had all operated on the torsion or tension principles, inherited from the Roman military engineers. They were not accurate. With the trebuchet, however, it was possible to estimate the exact weight of stone in the cassion, and correlate this with the length of the beam and with the weight of the stone about to be fired. These stone missiles could also be manufactured to a standard size. As a result, the trebuchet could be relied on to keep hitting a specified area of the curtain wall.

The defenders, meantime, would not have been idle. They might have constructed a strong palisade to seal off the breach once it was made, or they might have decided to retire to the inner bailey and pour down fire from the flanking towers as the attackers rushed in. In this case the attack would have to start its siege operations all over again to break into the inner bailey.

The new-style castle was not a passive fortification. It was provided with postern gates, through which a resolute commander could conduct surprise sorties which might catch the besiegers unawares. The barbican was a great help in allowing units of the defenders to move in and out of the castle without imperiling the central defence area. A wise attacker was constantly on his guard to prevent his siege works being burnt and destroyed. A skilfully defended castle was a hornet's nest to be approached with caution.

Finally the attacking commander might decide to take the great risk of trying to storm the wall with scaling ladders, or with using a mobile tower called the Belfry. The latter device has fixed itself in popular imagination as the chief offensive weapon in the siege warfare of the Middle Ages. Viollet-le-Duc, the great 19th century French architect who reconstructed the chateau of Pierrefonds for Napoleon III and practically rebuilt the walls of Carcassonne, published his "Annals of a Fortress" in which he gave a thrilling account, based on a great knowledge of mediaeval military architecture, of an imaginary assault by the Belfry on a typical "new-style" castle of Eastern France. The illustrations fixed themselves firmly in the mind. You could visualise this tall, three-storied timber tower, built to overtop the walls, being levered slowly forward on rollers, with the armed men packing the upper storey ready to leap forward as the assault bridge dropped across the battlements. The device looked almost as dangerous to the assailants as to the men waiting to repel them. We have vivid descriptions of the use of belfries in the Siege of Acre during the Third Crusade, but in the end they proved unsuccessful.

Just over seventy years later we have an equally vivid account of the siege of Kenilworth Castle by young Prince Edward - later Edward I, and the Hammer of the Welsh as well as of the Scots. This siege followed the defeat and death of Simon de Montfort at the battle of Evesham. It went on for six months, for Kenilworth had recently been refortified on a big scale and was surrounded in parts by a lake of more than a hundred acres in extent. The chronicle of Mathew of Westminster describes how numerous engines were set up outside the walls, to be countered by the engines constructed by the besieged. If Mathew is to be believed it sometimes occurred that stones hurled from either side smashed against each other in the air. Prince Edward pressed on with the construction of a great tower, but this last attempt to over-top the walls came to grief. In the long run Kenilworth surrendered, but only because the garrison had been weakened by disease and lack of food. This was the usual outcome of so many successful mediaeval sieges - the garrison was not overwhelmed by the techniques of the attackers but gave up for political reasons or because they were not relieved. The castle defenders were always gazing out from their battered walls in the hope of seeing the approaching banners of the relieving force marching to their rescue. They could hold out for a long time but not indefinitely. Sooner or later starvation was inevitable. Kenilworth surrendered because there was no-one on the de Montfort side who could raise an army to come to its rescue.

There were two extremely interested men present at this memorable siege. Among the defenders was a cleric named Master Peris from Radnor, who combined the job of surgeon with that of chaplain. He gave such heart to the men by his example that he was hailed as "the stalwardest clerk in all England", but we note that he came from the Welsh Marches, where men had long practice in this business of defending castles.

The second interested man was young Gilbert de Clare, Earl of Gloucester and Lord of Glamorgan. Three years later he was going to plan a castle that would eclipse all castles hitherto constructed in Britain, one which was going to embody every new defensive trick and which remains today the largest castle in the land with the exception of Windsor. In 1268 the foundations of the castle were laid on the selected site at Caerphilly, 7 miles north of Cardiff. Two years later they were torn up by the Welsh. Undaunted De Clare decided to built on an epic scale. At Kenilworth he had seen the defensive value of large sheets of water, so his new military masterpiece at Caerphilly would be surrounded by even vaster lakes. He had also realised the need for a series of defensive circles, one within the other, each one stronger and higher than the last. So he, or rather his master builder, created Wales's first and biggest Concentric Castle.

The concentric castle was the climax of the centuries-long development of the art of fortification in stone before the advent of gun-powder. We have seen how the simple curtain wall had been strengthened by the addition of round towers at regular intervals; how the round donjon had replaced the square one; how the keep itself had been regulated to an obscure role as the defence moved forward to an active role centred around the great gatehouse; how the simple bailey might be divided into two and how the barbican was introduced to add a further obstacle to the complicated steeple-chase over a series of stone walls that the castle now represented. One more step remained to be taken. Why not put a second "enceinte" inside the first. If you made this second enceinte higher than the first, then the defenders of the outer circuit can be reinforced by the fire-power of those on the inner walls. Anyone who succeeded in crossing the outer wall would find himself caught in the killing ground between the walls. If you then surrounded the outer circuit with a wide moat, and added a strong barbican to protect the drawbridge and causeway that led to the first gatehouse on the outer circuit you might at last have achieved the mediaeval architect's dream. You might have built the impregnable castle! When you look at Caerphilly you begin to feel that here, on a low-lying site among the hills behind Cardiff the dream has indeed come true. If this castle had been built in some convenient spot near London it would have long ago become one of Britain's show places. Instead it is tucked away over the hills, north of Cardiff, on the edge of the coalfield. Nevertheless it makes an overpowering impression on first sight. When Tennyson saw it in full decay he declared, "this is not a castle, it is a whole ruined town". Since then the ruins have been put into order. First the indispensible third Marquis of Bute, and then his son, saved the threatened walls and now the Department of the Environment has restored the moats to their full glory. Today Caerphilly can give you a splendid picture of what a concentric castle looked like in its heyday. True the towers are roofless and one was blown up, probably during the "slighting" of the castle after the Civil Wars; but so carelessly that it leans at an angle which local opinion takes pride in maintaining is greater than that of the Leaning Tower of Pisa. Yet the general impression remains of the power and ingenuity of the concentric idea.

Earl Gilbert deliberately chose a low lying site on the little Nant-y-Gledyr brook. Undoubtedly he remembered the great lake at Kenilworth and was determined to create an even bigger one. Across the brook an enormous dam was built, which was developed in stages into what is now known as the South and North Platforms. In the centre of the barrier was a great gateway, itself approached over a double

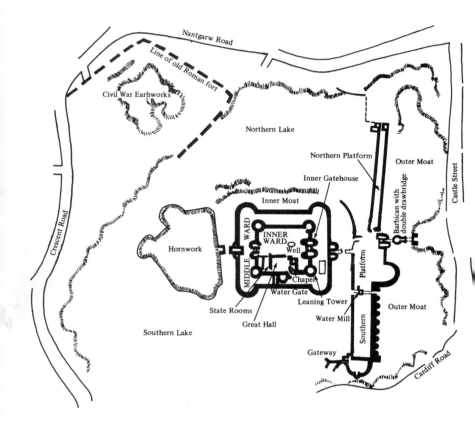

Sketch-plan of Caerphilly

drawbridge with a small barbican in the middle. Before the barrier was a wide, wet moat. The north section of the barrier could be cut off from the south barrier by a series of ingenious canals and gaps. At the far end stood two towers guarding the point where the barrier and the outer moat came to an end. They were entered from the wall walk over a series of "oubliettes"—pits covered by trap doors. These traps could be sprung by the garrison if compelled to retreat along the wall. The north platform, like the south, was undefended on its inner side. Any enemy who crossed the outer wall would be under fire from the inner wards beyond. The south platform also ended in towers guarding the main sluice controlling the water levels and the water mill, worked in time of peace by the running water. Here also was the south gateway leading to the little town that grew up in the shelter of the castle. The whole of these barrier towers and platforms can be regarded as a gigantic realisation of the barbican principle, since a complete concentric castle still lay beyond this impressive construction.

The central castle within a castle consists of two circuits of walls and towers, one inside the other. As the concentric idea demanded, the inner circuit was far higher than the outer to enable the defenders to double their fire. The inner ward contained the heart of the castle. Here was the noble Great Hall and the Eastern Gatehouse. The gatehouse was one of the finest features of Caerphilly. The gatehouse passage was fitted with the usual portcullis. The roof of the passage was pierced with the regulation "murder holes" for throwing down missiles and in addition, a large chute which allowed even more unpleasant surprises to be dropped on the attackers. The gatehouse also contained, on the second floor, the spacious hall used by the Constables together with a small chapel. In the centre of the inner ward was the well. The whole of the inner and outer wards were surrounded by the widest part of the lakes. From the great hall a covered passage led down through the wards to a small water gate which could act as a postern.

Even then the builders were not satisfied. Out in the lake to the west of the western gateway to the outer ward, and again reached by a drawbridge, they placed an artificial island known as a Horn-work. Its sides were revetted and it probably carried a wooden palisade. It fulfilled the same function as a barbican - a device for softening the first blow of an attack. Although, as you look at Caerphilly rising out of the waters of the moat beyond the hornwork, you are bound to ask "Who would be mad enough to try and assault the castle from this side?"

But as you gaze at the huge bastions, the vast lakes and the forest of towers mirrored in the water, two other questions are bound to puzzle your imagination. Where did the concentric idea come from originally? And why was this particular castle built on such a gigantic scale? To answer the first question we must travel to look at a building nearly 2000 miles from Caerphilly.

In the arid mountainous country on the border between the modern Syria and Northern Lebanon stands the great fortress of Krak-des-Chevaliers. Although it is perched on a high steep hill and not in a low valley, here, unmistakably, is the fore-runner of the central section of Caerphilly castle. Here are the same massive round towers, the complex barbican and winding approaches, a deep dry ditch instead of a wet moat, but above all, one circuit of walls place within the other so that the inner completely dominates the outer. Krak was built by the great military orders of the Hospitallers to protect the Marches (as it were) of Outremer. These were the lands of Palestine captured from the Moslems by the early crusaders - again a parallel with the advance of the Normans in the Welsh borderland. But incredible as it may seem to anyone looking at Krak today, it fell to a direct assault by the Sultan Baibars and his Mameluk Army. After a bombardment they broke into the outer enceinte. It took them a fortnight to crack the inner enceinte and even then the survivors of the defence held out for ten more days in one of the towers. The garrison must have been too small for a proper defence, for by the time of this siege the whole land of Outremer was at the end of its tether and had few more years to live. The defenders would also have been discouraged from the start by the knowledge that there was no hope of that supreme morale builder for castle garrisons - the advance of a relieving force. The date of the fall of Krak was March,1271, the very time when young Gilbert de Clare was building the foundations of his new Welsh masterpiece after the destruction of his earlier attempt at fortification in Caerphilly by the Welsh prince Llywelyn. In May of the same year, Prince Edward of England, afterwards Edward I, landed at Acre to fulfil his crusader's vow. He was one of the last of the great men of Europe to think it worth doing so.

There were other concentric castles in Outremer and visiting crusaders must have been familiar with them, for the crusading movement went on for nearly two hundred years at the very time when the new-type castle was developing in Europe; when the donjon was being relegated to the rear of the defence; when the gatehouse was being strengthened; when the curtain wall was provided with outflanking round towers, and finally when the concentric plan was coming into favour. Was this development the direct result of the Crusades and the lessons learnt in the struggle for the defence of the Holy Land? It is tempting to think so. The idea of an inner and outer line of fortification is clearly foreshadowed for all to see in the great walls of Constantinople. Nothing is more moving in the literature of the Crusades than Villehardouin's description of the amazement of the men of the Fourth Crusade in 1204, when their fleet sailed towards the great capital of the East, and they saw the white glittering city and its mighty double wall rising before them above the blue waters of the Bosphorus. True the Crusaders then proceeded to sack this Christian city with gusto, but they were still dazzled by what they saw. The theme of the multiangular walls of Constantinople will re-occur almost a hundred years later when Edward I built his castle of Caernarfon in far distant North Wales.

There was no question, too, that the Byzantines were the heirs to the military science of Rome and that the pressure on them had continued for hundreds of years, forcing them to keep on developing their own ideas on warfare. The Crusaders were bound to learn many things from them, especially in the field of the complicated stone throwing machines used in attacking castles. The Arabs learnt from them too, but were never so interested in defence as in attack. Their armies were essentially planned for mobility. But the typical Byzantine castle was also designed with an eye on mobile war. Byzantine strategists assumed that there would always be a large fund of manpower to draw on, and although their castles were liberally supplied with towers and earthworks, the buildings were not required to be the ultimate strongpoints. As Sir Stephen Runciman summed it up in his magisterial history of the Crusades, "The Byzantine castle was not much more than a fortified camp . . . designed to deal with an enemy whose armaments were less formidable than the Byzantines . . . The Commander was a professional soldier who left his wife and children at home". Sir Stephen concludes, "The main use of the castle was as barracks. It was inconvenient to force the soldiers to toil up and down a mountain every time they moved".

The Frankish settlers of Outremer needed other qualities in their castles. Like the Lords Marcher of Wales they were living on a frontier and they were comparatively small in numbers. Their castles had to be administrative centres, secure dwelling places, strong-boxes for their money and arsenals for their weapons. They needed fortresses which could be defended by small numbers of efficient professionals. Again the same conditions obtained in the Marches of Wales. The garrisons could be surprisingly small in some of the greatest of Welsh castles. Pembroke, in 1252, was held by two mounted men and ten soldiers. Their numbers could naturally be increased in time of serious trouble. Most astonishingly of all, when Caerphilly itself was surrendered for political reasons in 1327 after the longest siege in its history, only 137 men marched out under the Constable, John de Felton. They included such stalwart warriors as Eustace the Cook, William the Baker, John the Smith, John the Tailor and John the Waiter, but who probably contributed as much to the morale of the defence as many a fighting soldier.

Small garrisons needed help from the military architects, who obliged by developing even more elaborate schemes of defence. Many modern students of mediaeval building have suggested that a lot of those elaborate innovations were unnecessary - that it didn't make any real difference if your castle towers were round, rectangular or shaped like a spur and that as long as your walls were thick, your gatehouse solid and your whole defensive system placed on a rock, you were in business. It has also been claimed that all the later refinements of castle building including the concentric idea, could have developed naturally in Europe itself.

But Krak was built before Caerphilly, and Outremer could be regarded as the most far flung of Europe's frontiers. A frontier has always been a place for testing new ideas. The Franks on the frontier of the Holy Land may not have got all their new defensive tricks from their experience in the East, but it was they who developed the winding approach to the entrance of the gateway later favoured by the Arabs. The Byzantines used their castles not only as military camps but as storehouses for their big assault machines. They had therefore no desire to complicate the exits. But wherever the new ideas came from, the Franks in the Holy Land had every opportunity of trying them out under the most rigorous conditions, and the result of this experience must certainly have been known in the West.

When de Clare came to build Caerphilly, his architect or master-builder could draw on all the latest ideas then circulating among his colleagues, and right nobly did he exploit and develop them. But now comes a second series of questions. Why was Caerphilly built on such a scale? What need was there to construct a castle which far exceeded in size and elaboration any so far constructed in Wales and which rivalled any then being built in the whole of Europe? What new danger threatened the rich lands of Glamorgan which had now been firmly in Marcher hands for nearly two hundred years? To understand the purpose of Caerphilly - and several other Welsh castles that were being hurriedly reconstructed at this time - we must return from distant Palestine.

In the next chapter we must make a quick survey of the Welsh scene in the first half of the 13th century. We will then discover how politics forced the Marcher barons and the Welsh princes to begin a new era of elaborate castle building.

RAGLAN. The 15th-century machicolations are the finest in the country.

CAREW. The castle opens its windows to the peace of the Tudors.

5

The Two Llywelyns

We have seen how Wales had survived the first powerful onrush of the original Norman invaders, and how the Norman barons - or the Anglo-Normans as we should perhaps now call them - had nevertheless firmly established themselves in some of the most desirable parts of the country. As the 13th century dawned, Wales was seen to be clearly divided into two.

In the North and the West there were still independent Welsh rulers. They had to pay homage to the King of England, but they governed their principalities according to Welsh law, fought and made alliances amongst themselves, and struggled, on the whole with success, to keep the Marcher barons out of their territories. This Welsh heartland, or Pura Wallia in the Mediaeval Latin of the law-courts, was divided into three parts, each with its own character and traditional policy. In the North and North-West was Gwynedd. The core of this principality was the complex of mountains which form the Snowdonia National Park today - the wilds of Snowdon itself and the equally rugged country of Ardudwy and the area around Cader Idris, which now are part of modern Merionethshire. Its Southern boundary touched the mouth of the river Dovey. To the North of this mountain land was the Island of Anglesey, low-lying, and so fertile that it rejoiced in the title of "Mon, Mam Cymru" - Anglesey, the Mother of Wales. This

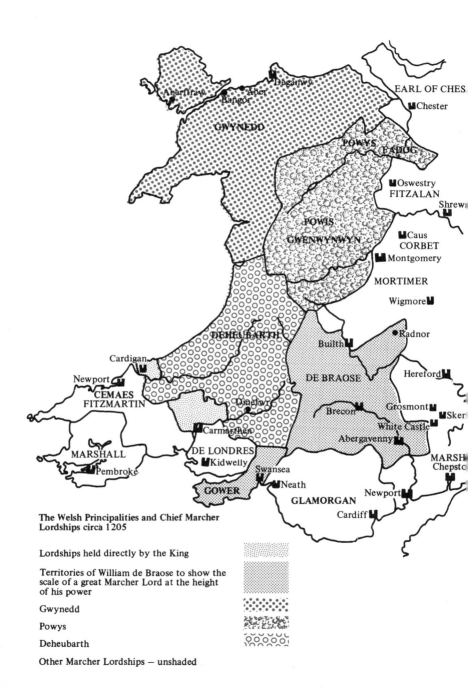

The Welsh Principalities and Chief Marcher
Lordships circa 1205

Lordships held directly by the King

Territories of William de Braose to show the
scale of a great Marcher Lord at the height
of his power

Gwynedd

Powys

Deheubarth

Other Marcher Lordships — unshaded

combination of mountain fastness and rich granary gave Gwynedd its strength, especially as the mountains plunged precipitously down to the sea at Llanfairfechan and sealed off any approach to Anglesey by land. The river Conway and its valley could be regarded as a strong moat just east of this mountain curtain-wall. Inner Gwynedd was a natural fortress which required siege methods to force. East of the Conway the land was more open to invasion and counter-invasion. The fertile Vale of Clwyd and the low plain of Flint at the mouth of the estuary of the Dee were always a point of dispute. Historically they were part of Gwynedd. But when the rulers of Gwynedd were weak, there was a danger that part of this territory would slip out of their grasp. As the 13th century dawned Gwynedd was at the beginning of the most glorious and eventually the most tragic period in its history. All the territory to the East of the Conway was firmly under its control.

South of Gwynedd lay Powys. It touched the sea at the mouth of the Dovey, but otherwise it was an inland principality, embracing the valley of the Dee and the Valley of the Upper Severn and its tributaries. Geographically it was the most vulnerable of all the Welsh territories. These wide valleys led deep into the hills. There was no hard core like Snowdonia into which the rulers could retreat, no Anglesey to help feed the beleaguered garrison. Some of the lands of Powys were very exposed indeed. Maelor stretched across the Dee well out into the flat meadows of the Cheshire plain. Any ruler of Powys had to be unadventurous and conciliatory. He had to exist by the kind permission of the King of England. The Princes of Powys earn very few marks from historians who take a totally nationalistic view. Again and again they were found coming hurriedly to terms with the English power. Not an heroic role - but Powys eventually survived when Gwynedd crashed into ruin. It may be that he who bends at the right time serves his country better than he who resists at the wrong time!

South West Wales formed the principality of Deheubarth. This area had suffered most from Norman pressure. But it staged a remarkable revival towards the end of the 12th century under the Lord Rhys, who, for a period of twenty-five years, made Deheubarth the most important principality in Wales. His was the power that forced his Norman neighbours in the southern Marches to spend their money on radically improving their castles. When this skilful and highly successful prince died in 1197, his sons immediately indulged in the fatal Welsh habit of squabbling over their inheritance. Deheubarth lost its pre-eminence. The immediate future, on the Welsh side, lay with Gwynedd.

Around these three Welsh principalities of Pura Wallia lay the ring of lands belonging to the Lords Marcher. Their boundaries had now been stabilised after a hundred years of border conflict. In some respects, both sides had learned to tolerate if not always to live peacefully with each other. There had been intermarriage between the noble Welsh and the Anglo–Normans. The Marches were no longer a raw borderland. The great Marcher families ran their huge estates almost like little kingdoms. They zealously guarded their private courts where the Law of the March was administered, not the Welsh law nor the King's Justice. No law books of this private Marcher law have come down to us. But, on the other hand, the Welsh laws were being intensively studied and coded around this period. In England great lawyers like Bracton were clarifying the practice of the royal courts. The law of the March depended a great deal on a mixture of custom, of survivals from the Welsh law originally administered in the territory and borrowings from the royal courts, tempered by the Lord Marcher's own idiosyncratic notions. It was by no means always unacceptable to those who lived under it.

This independence made any Lord Marcher who accumulated a number of Marcher estates a very powerful man indeed. William de Breos, who began his career with the notorious massacre at Abergavenny, accumulated so many lordships that he dominated the politics of the March for nearly thirty years. His fall and exile under King John in 1208 shook the whole of Wales. A more sympathetic baron was William Marshall the Elder. He was that unusual figure amongst the Lords Marcher, a self-made man. He was a penniless younger son of a comparatively minor baron who began his career at the court of the Connetable de Tancarville in Normandy, and he owed his early success to his amazing skill in tournaments. This ritualistic mock-combat was invented in Northern France by Geoffrey de Preuilly and immediately became popular throughout Western Europe. The tournament fulfilled an important need for the baronial class. It gave the knight practice in the business of war, which was the chief reason for his existence, under glamorous and, in many cases, lucrative circumstances. These early tournaments were rough affairs. You had to be skilful to survive. Young William soon swept the board. He travelled around the country with what could only be described as a team of professionals, rather like the tennis circus of today. His greatest stroke of luck came when the eldest son of Henry II, known as the Young King, became tournament mad. Henry II naturally got worried about financing his son on the professional tournament circuit, especially as the prize money usually came from the paying of a ransom or the forfeiting of his armour by an unsuccessful knight. The ransom of a King's son would be no light charge on the royal funds! The King put William in control of his son's team and he proved to be a brilliant team manager. Through the contacts with the great made at tournaments, William rose fast and high. Finally, he scooped the biggest prize of all - the hand of the heiress of Richard de Clare. This brought him all the great de Clare holdings in Glamorgan, Gwent and Pembroke, as well as their huge claims in Ireland. No modern sportsman or even cinema star could better a reward on this scale. William, at a stroke, became one of the greatest of the Marcher Lords. If we are to believe everything in the rhymed biography composed by his admiring minstrel after William's death in 1219, he was a paragon of Knighthood. Certainly he behaved well in Wales, and the great round keep of Pembroke Castle can stand as his memorial.

But carefully watching the Marshalls, the de Clares, the Mortimers and the de Breoses were the men who were always prepared to interfere in the affairs of the March whenever a favourable chance presented itself - the Kings of England. The Norman and Plantagenet Kings were well aware of the dangers inherent in their over-powerful subjects. As so often happens in politics, the temporary arrangements of the period immediately succeeding the Conquest had turned into a permanent problem a hundred years later. Whenever possible the English Kings used the minorities of Marcher heirs to gain some temporary control over their territories. Henry I had become a Marcher baron himself when he got complete control of Carmarthen. John was lucky too. In the troubles that followed the death of the Lord Rhys, one of his sons, Maelgwyn, needing help in his difficulties, turned to the King. The Chronicler of Strata Florida records for 1199. "In this year, Maelgwyn ap Rhys sold to the English Aberteifi (Cardigan), the key of Wales, for a trifling sum, and this by reason of his fear and hatred of his brother Gruffydd." The Welsh execrated Maelgwyn but the Crown had got a very useful strong point for further interference in Welsh affairs. In the reign of John that interference provoked a remarkable and successful reaction.

Again we see the operation of the principle that England's difficulties were Wales's opportunities. In the very period when John had started to take Pura Wallia, Welsh Wales, firmly in hand, his troubles increased with his barons. As the 13th century developed, it became clear that North Wales had produced a man who would know how to take advantage of this trouble to the full. Llywelyn ap Iorwerth, the grandson of Owain Gwynedd, got power in the usual way of Welsh princes bedevilled by the dividing rule of Welsh inheritance - he seized it from his uncle. He proved to be the greatest and most constructive Welsh statesman of the Middle Ages. He survived all the pressure brought upon him by John, allied himself with the discontented barons, and saw to it that the redress of Welsh grievances had a prominent place in Magna Carta itself. By conquest, and then by tact and skilful negotiation, he became the acknowledged ruler of the whole of Pura Wallia. For the first time since the Norman invasion, all parts of the country administered under Welsh law were also united under one power. The Marcher barons had cause to fear Llywelyn.

In the course of his long and successful reign Llywelyn set himself out to create the sort of centralised feudal state that was developing so successfully during this period in France and England. He, too, had his body of devoted lawyers and civil servants. His state was held together firmly by the ties of homage and fealty. He and his successors strove to break the old destructive Welsh practice of the equal division of inheritance among all male heirs and to substitute for it the principle of single succession by the eldest son. The first Llywelyn succeeded in getting his son David acknowledged as sole heir by the whole of Pura Wallia. It was bad luck that David died without an heir seven years after he had succeeded to the total inheritance of his father. Llywelyn's work had to be done again. Yet so firmly had the foundations been laid, that by the middle of the 13th century his grandson, Llywelyn ap Gruffydd, was able to re-establish his power and even extend it still further into some of the great Marcher lordships. He could assume the proud title of Prince of Wales.

This Wales of the two Llywelyns was not the romantic tribal mountain fastness inhabited by poor but proud pastoralists which earlier 19th century writers delighted to depict. Modern research has produced a far different picture. One authority has roundly declared: "The epithet 'tribal', in the sense that it has been used hitherto of Wales, is inappropriate, and, as defined by modern anthropologists, is so vague that its use is best avoided in Celtic contexts." Wales, it appears, was much in line with the rest of Europe. It had its bondsmen firmly tied to the soil, its percentage of freemen who appeared comparatively late on the scene, and its aristocracy grouped around the central authority of the Prince. Pura Wallia, under the Llywelyns, was developing as an independent entity side by side with England. The Prince

of Wales would do homage to the King of England for his
principality as a whole, but he would firmly reject any direct
interference in its normal affairs.

When officials of King Edward I sent a peremptory letter
to Llywelyn ap Gruffydd forbidding him to construct a
castle with a market before it near the modern village of
Abermule, Llywelyn firmly replied that "the rights of his
principality are entirely separate from the rights of the
King's realm although he holds his principality under the
King's power . . . and the King has heard and in part seen
that Llywelyn's ancestors and himself had the power within
their boundaries to build and construct castles . . . without
prohibition by anyone."

Indeed, this was true. Over the last hundred years the
Welsh, as well as the Marcher barons and the King, had built
their castles. They had not applied to any English monarch
for 'licence to castellate'. The Welsh castles may not have
been quite as elaborate as those erected by their enemies - in
the long run Pura Wallia was not so rich as the Marches, but
they were' important nevertheless.

The principal seats of the two Llywelyns were not castles.
On the island of Anglesey, Aberffraw was their favourite
residence. Llywelyn the Great was proud to style himself
"Prince of Aberffraw and Lord of Snowdonia". Nothing
remains of his residence and the great hall of richly decorated wood which was its glory. A modern memorial in slate
placed on the bridge at Aberffraw is all that now reminds us
that it was once an important centre of power.

On the mainland the Llywelyns favoured Aber, not far
from Bangor and within reach of the main crossing over the
Menai Straits. Again nothing remains of the residence.
There is a motte at the foot of the high hills, but this may date
from the early days of Norman penetration in these parts. By
tradition Aber was the scene of one of the most dramatic
incidents in the life of Llywelyn the Great. Llywelyn had
married Joan, a natural daughter of King John, for marry-
ing into a royal family, even into an illegitimate section of it,
was a recognised way of aspiring to higher rank oneself. In

one of the most successful of his border wars the Prince had
captured William de Braos, the son of the famous - or in-
famous - de Braos disgraced by John. In 1230, after a period
of captivity, William was released to return on oath with his
ransom. But he had apparently used his period of captivity to
start an affair with Llywelyn's wife. When William returned he lost no time in renewing the illicit contact.
Llywelyn's suspicions were aroused. He caught the guilty
pair in each other's arms. There was only one thing that
Llywelyn could do. All Wales had a score to settle with the
scion of the hated house of de Braos. Eight hundred men
gathered on May 2nd, 1230, and, as the Abbot of Vaudrey reported, "at a certain manor called 'Crokein' he was made
'crogyn' " (that is hung on a tree). Public opinion, not only
in Pura Wallia but in the Marches as well, was firmly on
Llywelyn's side. It is pleasant after this to find that he eventually forgave his wife and she was buried with honour near
Llanfaes, in Anglesey, where Llywelyn established a house
of Franciscan friars to pray for her soul.

Neither Aberffraw or Aber seems to have been strongly defended or fortified. Here the rulers of Gwynedd dwelt in
peace surrounded by their rich manors. Their castles lay elsewhere, on their borders or in the final refuge of Snowdonia.
Most of the castles built by the Welsh in South Wales have
been altered out of all recognition or rebuilt completely at a
later date. The present castle of Dinefwr, the ancient seat of
the Lord Rhys, is 13th century and later - with the possible
exception of the round keep. But in North Wales we still
have examples which allow us to see the sort of fortification
built by the Welsh in the age of the Llywelyns.

At Dolwyddelan, on a rocky crest above the upper reaches
of the tumbling stream of the Lledr, is one of the oldest and
most picturesque of the Welsh castles. It probably consisted
originally of an irregular enclosure crowning the hill top defended by a wooden stockade or simple, dry-stone wall. The
most prominent feature today is the ruined keep, a strong,
square tower dating from the first half of the 13th century
and of a type familiar in many castles of South Wales of this

period. Here, according to tradition, Llywelyn the Great was born, but it is more likely that this event which occurred in 1173, took place at an earlier castle site which has recently been identified nearby. In the early years of Llywelyn's reign the stockade was replaced by a stone curtain. A second tower was erected later (possibly after the capture of the castle by the English) in the north-west angle of the curtain. The entrance to the castle was placed in the curtain wall, beside the keep. The entrance to the keep, itself, was protected by a drawbridge in a small forebuilding. Compared with the South Wales castles of the period, Dolwyddelan is naturally on a smaller scale. The courtyard measures 90 ft. in all directions. Gwynedd, even at its most prosperous, could not muster the resources of a Gilbert de Clare and certainly not those of the Kings of England. But Dolwyddelan, on its crag, was a strong castle nevertheless.

This pattern of a keep, a curtain wall and a second tower is repeated in other Welsh castles. Ewloe in Flintshire is particularly interesting since the castle fell into disuse immediately after Edward I had conquered Wales, and its design can be seen unaltered. It lies in what seems a curiously vulnerable site, on a densely wooded spur overlooking the level coastal plain of the Dee. It was founded by Llywelyn ap Gruffydd c. 1256 and was clearly built as a strong check on the nearby castle of Hawarden, the outlying defence of the Earldom of Chester.

The apsidal or round-ended keep at Ewloe was a typically Welsh feature which was formerly to be seen at Castell y Bere and elsewhere. It is still known as the Welsh Tower. The curtain wall that surrounds the enceinte is without flanking towers, but again there is a single strong tower at the edge of the spur. Ewloe in its prime might not have been so overlooked as it seems today since the level of the surrounding land may have been raised by siege works.

A third Welsh-built castle lay at Cricieth. This was founded by Llywelyn the Great as an important residence and a permanent depot for mobilising his military resources in the commote, or administrative unit, of Eifionydd.

Today the castle is concentric, with an inner ring built under Edward I. The original castle consisted of the outer circuit only with the principal accommodation in a strong rectangular tower, and a simple gateway in the curtain without the two flanking towers which were to become a normal feature in the larger castles of Wales. In Cricieth it is only the inner gateway that conforms to the new style. A remarkable feature of the outer circuit of Cricieth is the Engine Tower, called the "Gynnetwr" in a document of 1343. Its masonry is clearly of the same period as the rest of the outer circuit. It is one of the few towers in Wales which we know carried a great stone-throwing machine, or else a catapult or springald. Maybe the tower was adapted to this use after being remodelled under English occupation, although the Welsh had siege engines as well.

Dolbadarn, in the very heart of Snowdonia at Llanberis, must be the most photographed of all the native Welsh castles. It stands on a rocky knoll between the two Llanberis lakes with Snowdon itself as a background. It conforms to the Dolwyddelan pattern but is unique in having, as its main defence, a round not a square keep. Further south, in a valley that runs deep into Cader Idris, is a castle that can rival Dolbadarn in splendour of site - Castell y Bere. Its outlines have been carefully conserved by the Department of the Environment after it had fallen into utter ruin. It was probably built by Llewelyn the Great after 1221, when he deprived his son Gruffydd of Ardudwy and Meirionydd and wanted to demonstrate his hold on all the lands of Pura Wallia to the south. Again we have the same pattern as at Cricieth and Ewloe, with a strong inner keep and a gateway without flanking towers. Still, Castell y Bere on its high rock with an approach along a narrow, rocky ridge had no need of such refinements. Its site made it formidable.

These castles of the Princes of Gwynedd were not crudely built copies of contemporary English or Marcher constructions. They had a style of their own. Their best stoneworks was fine-cut. At Castell y Bere and at Cricieth, the central towers were decorated with sculptured stones, of

which can be seen in the National Museum of Wales at
Cardiff. Little remains of some of the other castles built by
the two Llywelyns, including Castell Carn Dochan behind
Llanuwchllyn at the top end of Bala Lake, and Dolforwyn,
the castle near Abermule in Montgomeryshire so defiantly
built by Llywelyn the Last, against the protests of Edward I's
officials.

The Princes of Powys, too, had their castles, but again the
remains are fragmentary; although the castle at Pool must
have been substantial, since the records of a siege of 1196
show that, after vainly trying to scale the walls, the English
successfully broke into the castle by undermining.

Dinas Bran, guarding the entrance to the upper valley of
the Dee, at Llangollen, is only a picturesque fragment today.
No doubt more of its plans will be revealed when it has been
systematically excavated.

It was the castles of the Llywelyns however, which
showed that a powerful and well-organised state had now
been created in Wales; a state, moreover, whose growth posed
a growing threat to the Marcher Barons. The threat became
even more serious in 1267. In that year the Treaty of Montgomery was signed between Llywelyn ap Gruffydd and
Henry III. Llywelyn had supported Simon de Montfort, but
his position was unshaken by de Montfort's death in the
Battle of Evesham. Henry III and his advisors were anxious
to obtain permanent peace in England and were prepared to
make large concessions in Wales. Llywelyn was acknowledged Prince of Wales. He was to hold not only Pura Wallia
(the three Welsh Principalities of Gwynedd, Powys and
Deheubarth) but great tracts of the Marcher lordships as
well. At the expense of the Mortimers and the de Bohuns he
received land all along the middle March, and also became
possessed of Builth in the upper Wye valley and Brecon on
the upper Usk. This last lordship brought Llywelyn into
direct contact with the lordship of Glamorgan and so with
Gilbert de Clare, Earl of Gloucester and Lord of Glamorgan.

For the first time for many a long year the de Clares had to face a serious challenge to their power in Glamorgan. By the treaty of Montgomery all Welsh barons were now to hold their lands directly from the Prince of Wales. This clause was ambiguous. The King and the Papal Legate who had acted as mediator for the treaty clearly meant it to refer to the Welsh barons now under Llywelyn's direct rule, but it was impossible for Llywelyn to interpret it as giving him rights over all rulers of Welsh origin, even when they had long been subject to Marcher lords. The temptation to Llywelyn to interfere in the affairs of Glamorgan was irresistible . The rulers of the commote of Senghenydd, covering the hill-lands of north-east Glamorgan, had long been under the suzerainty of the de Clare lordship. But they were Welsh. Llywelyn could now maintain that Senghenydd should owe allegiance to him. If this claim were allowed, Llywelyn's power would sweep southward to within seven miles of the great de Clare stronghold of Cardiff and the rich plainlands of the Vale of Glamorgan.

This was intolerable to the Lord of Glamorgan. De Clare even anticipated the terms of the treaty of Montgomery in 1266 by dispossessing Gruffydd ap Rhys, the Welsh ruler of Senghenydd and packing him off to captivity in Ireland. On April 11, 1268, within six months of the signing of the treaty, the first foundations of the castle of Caerphilly were laid. Llywelyn countered by crossing the borders of the lordship of Brecon and moving into upper Senghenydd. There were complicated efforts at negotiation by the King. They broke down. Llywelyn then determined to forestall de Clare and, in October, 1270, burnt all the new castle works to the ground.

De Clare replied by starting to rebuild a second castle on an even bigger scale - the castle that we see today. He pushed the work forward at record speed. Llywelyn threatened a second attack and only withdrew when it was agreed that, pending arbitration, the new works as far as they had already been completed, should be placed temporarily in the hands of representatives of the Crown. The neutral keepers were the Bishops of Worcester and Lichfield. The ecclesiastics proved to be more efficient as bishops than as castellians. One bright morning in 1272, the Constable of the de Clare castle of Cardiff, accompanied by two knights, paid a friendly call on the Bishops' representatives at Caerphilly. He asked if his two companions could look in for a brief moment, one to check some stores left in the castle and the other to look over the armour. Unfortunately the unsuspicious Bishops' men left the gate open. Immediately the Constable and 40 soldiers who had been hidden near at hand, dashed in and took back the castle. An interesting demonstration that no amount of ingenuity in constructing a castle could guarantee that it would not be captured if the defenders were not active and alert! Llywelyn's fury can be imagined.

After this recapture the works went forward rapidly. We can now understand the reason for the scale of Caerphilly. There was going to be no conventional Marcher fortress. The threat represented by the Wales of Llywelyn ap Gruffydd demanded a reply on an heroic scale. De Clare was not the only Marcher who felt insecure. All along the March the seven years that followed the Treaty of Montgomery saw the barons looking to their defences. It is to this period that we owe the inner ring of the castle of Kidwelly. Roger Bigod built a new western gatehouse to Chepstow castle in the approved new style, and the years that followed 1212 saw the completion of the town wall there. Llywelyn ap Gruffydd appeared to be in the high tide of success. Never had the omens seemed brighter for an independent Principality of Wales.

But, in November 1272, the aged King Henry III died after one of the longest and most checkered reigns in English history. His heir, Edward, was still on his Crusade. Events awaited his return. But there were signs of danger ahead. Edward had already proved himself a man of outstanding skill in both the mock battle of the tournament and the realities of mediaeval war. The vision that Edward held in his mind of a Britain tidily grouped under the overlordship of the King of England conflicted totally with the semi-independent Wales which the two Llywelyn's had struggled to create. The clash, when it came, was to prove fatal to Llywelyn: and lead directly to the most remarkable, elaborate and expensive programme of castle building yet undertaken in Mediaeval Europe.

6

The Iron Ring

Edward I was now in the prime of life. He was an organiser, a legalist, a ruler inspired by high notions of his position and of the honour and glory he could bring to the
realm. To such a man, the very existence of semi-independent Celtic kingdoms and princedoms on his border was
"administratively untidy". He was bound, sooner or later, to
take a cool look at the activities of the Prince of Wales.
Llywelyn and his grandfather had been trying to do in Wales
exactly what Edward and his predecessors had been doing in
England during the 13th century - that is to create a powerful, centralised feudal state in which the King, his justice, his
taxes and his administration should be the undisputed
central power. This policy for Wales was unacceptable to
Edward who was now ready to carry his own policy of
centralisation to its logical conclusion. This he was in a position to do because he was now King of a united England.
The domestic struggles of the de Montfort period, which
had given Llywelyn such golden opportunities in 1267, were
over. Llywelyn would have been well advised to act caut-
iously.

This, however, is just what he did not do. He did not pay
Edward the annual sums he had bound himself to pay. He
announced his proposed marriage to - of all women -
Eleanor, the daughter of Edward's late, bitter enemy, Simon
de Montfort. And, most important and damaging of all, he
made every excuse to delay or even avoid his personal act of

homage to the king. This formal ceremony was most important in mediaeval eyes. The Prince of Wales had to be seen swearing his fealty to Edward in the presence of the baronage of England and Wales. The two Llywelyns had attached the same importance to similar acts of homage by the leading Welsh rulers to them, personally. It allowed them to claim undisputed rights and authority over the whole of the territories submitted to· them in Wales. It was vital for Llywelyn ap Gruffydd to check any tendency for the great Welsh or the Marcher barons under his control to try to swear their homage direct to the King. Maybe some fear of this kind was behind Llywelyn's strange persistence in refusing his own act of homage.

Edward was not the sort of man to let such an uncertain situation continue. His determination to attempt a solution of what he regarded as the Welsh problem was hardened when Llywelyn's brother David and Gruffydd ap Gwenwynwyn of Powys fled to him for protection after an abortive plot against the Prince of Wales. A show-down was now inevitable. Edward knew that he could expect support not only from the Marcher lords dispossessed by Llywelyn but from many of the leading barons in Pura Wallia itself. Llywelyn's internal position had weaknesses which had been disguised by his dazzling success after the Treaty of Montgomery. His hand had lain heavily on his own subordinates. He could not expect their undivided loyalty when the testing time came. It is easy, from the vantage point of the 20th century, to talks as if such men as David, Gruffydd ap Gwenwynwyn and Rhys ap Maredudd of Deheubarth were traitors to a national cause. Men did not think in the 13th century in terms of a national state on modern lines. The personal bond with the ruler was almost as important as being a Welshman or an Englishman, although a strong sense of community in .language and race was always present.

In the autumn of 1276, Edward began his war with Llywelyn. The Marcher barons made the preliminary moves, aided by the royal army. In Edward's strategy we see the importance he attached, from the very first, to the castles in the area of operations. He needed them as his strong bases for the advance of his armies in the field when spring brought the main campaigning season. Thus, by the end of the winter, his own units or those of the Marcher lords had cleared the way into Llywelyn's country at a series of important points. The castles of Chester and Montgomery were reinforced. In South Wales, the local forces moved up from the royal castle of Carmarthen along the Towy valley. Helped by Rhys ap Meredudd, they were able to capture Dinefwr and even lonely Carreg Cennen. Edward had secured his bases. To Chester then, all through the spring of 1277, fighting men and artisans were summoned from all over England. Edward arrived to take command in July.

In the south, the invaders moved on from the Dinefwr area, captured the castle of Llandovery, and then cut across to the Teifi. They marched down the Aeron valley and then up the coast to Aberystwyth, where they immediately started to build a castle. In mid-Wales Edward's levies pushed up the Severn, then crossed into the upper Wye valley. They began the construction of an elaborate castle at Builth. In North Wales, Edward himself led his forces along the coast. A big body of quarrymen, roadmakers, woodcutters and charcoal burners cleared the way through dense woodlands. Edward was as firm a believer in logistics as any American general of the last war. Acting on the celebrated U.S. principle, "In this army, we don't solve our problems, we overwhelm them!" Edward certainly overwhelmed Llywelyn. As soon as he occupied the sites he began building the castles of Flint at the mouth of the wide estuary of the Dee and Rhuddlan at the mouth of the Clwyd. These two bases were vital, the former a coastal stronghold which could be supplied by the fleet, while the latter had been the key to the North Wales coastal land route since prehistoric times. Rhuddlan had been, in addition, a royal seat of Gruffydd ap Llywelyn until the palace was burnt in 1063 and it was there that a motte-and-bailey castle had been thrown up by the Norman Robert of Rhuddlan in 1073.

In all past attempts to attack Gwynedd, the Welsh could count on the safe tactics of a final retreat to the Conway valley. Here, the solid wall of the Carneddau mountains came down to the sea and an invader could be held easily along this line. Even the modern roads and railway have to tunnel through the mountains to turn this formidable barrier. Beyond lay the fertile island of Anglesey where the Welsh would always have a source of supply. They could afford to stay on the Conway line until the winter rains came to their rescue. The Welsh could rely on the defensive power of heavy winter rain as confidently as the Russians relied on the oncoming of the snow against Napoleon and Hitler. Edward neutralised this Welsh advantage by bringing a fleet of 25 ships up from the Cinque Ports in the English channel. These tough seamen were experts in the naval warfare of their day. Llywelyn had nothing to match them. He had used ships in the past to counter threats from Ireland, but he could not compete with this powerful flotilla from the Cinque Ports.

Edward's army, with its attendant hordes of workmen, methodically pushed along the coast from Flint and up to Rhuddlan by the last weeks of August. Rhuddlan, at the point where the Clwyd was still tidal, could act as a port - the only one along this coastline until the Conway river itself. From Rhuddlan the fleet could sail across to Anglesey, and attack the cornlands of the island. This was a deadly thrust at the heart of the Welsh stronghold. Llywelyn had no option but to come to terms.

They were tough. By the Treaty of Aberconway the Prince of Wales kept his title but was confined to the original princedom of Gwynedd, that is to the hard core formed by Anglesey, Snowdonia, Lleyn and Meirionydd. David received land in the valley of the Clwyd, the princes of Powys returned and provision was made for Rhys ap Maredudd in Deheubarth. But the Marcher barons came back in force in Brecon and mid-Wales. Above all, the king held the bulk of the land yielded by Llywelyn. The royal power was now advanced along the North Wales coast to the banks of the

Conway, and was firmly established on the west coast and the upper Wye. Edward, in one stroke, had become, as it were, the greatest of the Lords Marcher.

His power was founded on the great castles now rising at the King's command. Aberystwyth, Builth, Flint and Rhuddlan were all begun by the Spring of 1278. Money on a big scale was expended. Rhuddlan in particular became a fortress of major importance. It is worth looking at closely since it would be the pattern for the succeeding fortresses that Edward would build later on after his final reckoning with Llywelyn in 1282. It was also the first masterpiece of the man whose name was to be so closely linked with Edward's castle building in Wales for over 30 years - Master James of St. George.

Here we can salute a very great master-builder indeed. He can stand side by side with such men as Hugh Herland who built the roof of Westminster Hall, Simon of Thirsk who created the Angel Choir at Lincoln, and even with the later royal master-builders and architects like Inigo Jones and Wren. For he was not only a magnificent organiser and administrator who could keep building projects moving on a big scale. He was a great artist as well. His castles in North Wales all show a genius for handling masses, for grouping towers into artistic arrangements that give a genuine visual excitement no matter how often you see them. These castles were, of course, extremely efficient machines for defence. They would never have been built otherwise. But they also possess that quality over and above mere utility that is the hall-mark of great architecture. The famous French engineer of the 17th century, Vauban, once exclaimed when he saw the tower of Coutances Cathedral, "Who was that sublime madman who dared to launch such a monument into the air ." We sense the same feeling of delighted astonishment when we look at the forest of tall towers sprouting from the walls of Conway, and see the walls of Caernarfon mirrored in the still waters of the Seiont. No two castles built by James of St. George were alike. His castles were no modern, mass-produced defensive slabs, rubber-stamped onto a protesting landscape. He possessed the supreme gift of exactly suiting the design to the site.

We see his castles today after centuries of neglect and pillage and they can still impress. How magnificent they must have looked in their prime with the walls made dazzling white with plaster and each tower crowned by a low, pointed roof, with banners waving to announce that their royal sponsor was perhaps, for the moment, in residence!

James was probably a Savoyard, and Edward met him when he went on his military pilgrimage to the Holy Land and stayed with his cousin, Philip of Savoy. James had already been sixteen years in the service of the Courts of Savoy and was a man of experience. He took his name from the castle he designed and built at St. Georges-d'Espéranche, south-east of Lyons. It is intriguing to note that this castle was distinguished by multiangular towers - a motive Master James was to repeat with such splendid effect at Caernarfon. He came in Edward's train when the king returned to England, and rose rapidly in favour to become eventually Master of the King's Work in Wales - in fact a sort of Albert Speer to Edward I! In the fashion of all the master-builders of the Middle Ages he must have brought the nucleus of his staff with him, since foreign names turn up from time to time in the records of his castle construction. We will be talking of Master James as being the architect for a whole series of castles, but we cannot be certain that he, individually, designed every one. He, however, was the man at the head of things. It is not unfair to give him the credit. No man could have been responsible for such an impressive scale of work without the backing of a large and experienced body of trained men, on whom he could rely. In Builth, Aberystwyth, Flint, and above all in Rhuddlan, we see Master James and his team getting to work for the first time in Wales.

First, the site was chosen on the steep banks of the Clwyd, away from the motte-and-bailey construction originally built by Robert of Rhuddlan. This mound, called the Twthill, is still there, a few hundred yards from the great, new construction that now started to rise with impressive speed. Rhuddlan was a concentric castle - Caerphilly had made its impression! The outer ward was surrounded by a deep dry ditch. The inner ward was a square with two entrances opposite each other, both guarded by double round towers. In the design of Rhuddlan we sense Master James delighting in an almost mathematical symmetry - a delight he was to repeat 15 years later when he came to build Beaumaris.

The Inner Ward was the administrative centre. The buildings were probably timber-framed, and thus few traces of them remain. They would have included the King's Hall and Chamber, the Queen's rooms and all the necessary accommodation for the officials and courtiers. The Constable of the castle, the man who was responsible for its garrison, would have had his headquarters in one of the gatehouses.

The Outer Ward was used as a base and a storehouse - here were the granary, the stables, a forge and the specialised workshops, including one for the Queen's goldsmith. Here, too, were stored the siege-engines, the artillery of the day, and their ammunition of specially rounded stones. Inside this safe circuit, the extra troops required for campaigning could be assembled. And to the Outer Ward provisions and war material could be brought in from the sea. The circuit led down to the river bank, where the quay was protected by a powerful line of walls ending in Gellot's Tower. Gellot was Gellot de Chalons, who we know was working at Conway in 1286. Was he among the experts who came over on the staff of Master James?

The quay was one of the basic reasons for the choice of the site of Rhuddlan. Edward's tactics needed the support of his fleet. He had to have a good harbour for his ships as far west as possible, and the lower reaches of the River Clwyd could give him one. The river, however, meandered in shallows over the low Marsh of Rhuddlan to the sea. Edward, therefore, undertook a major engineering work, astonishing in its scale. He cut a new, deep-water channel for the

Clwyd, for over two miles from the castle to the river mouth. A force of "fossatores", or ditch-diggers, was set to work. They kept at it for three years, until Edward had a canalised river which would accommodate ships up to 40 tons burden. The cost of this canal, together with the castle and the ancillary works, was nearly £10,000 in the money of the day. In terms of our own times this must have approached the £3,000,000 mark. And expenditure was going on at Flint and elsewhere at the same time. Castle building was an expensive business !

Nor was this all. At Flint and Rhuddlan Edward laid out a small town next to the castle, defended by earthen ramparts, and wooden palisades. This would be his common practice throughout his wars and his re-organisation of political arrangements in North Wales. These small boroughs were denied to the Welsh, at least at their inception. They were to be centres of English influence, where the help of officials, merchants and artisans could be enlisted in the taming of the newly won territories. The castle and the town were a unit, both created for the same purpose. As in so many of his building and political projects, Edward may have been influenced by what he had seen on the continent. In 1270 he had embarked for his Crusade at Aigues-Mortes, the new town or "bastide" built by St. Louis on the marshes at the mouth of the Rhone. These "bastides" were deliberately created by royal policy, and were regularly laid out, with their governing body appointed by royal authority. The "bastide" supplied the perfect model for Edward's new towns. We even see echoes of Aigues-Mortes in their architecture. Anyone looking along the line of the water front of the little French town, from which the sea has now retreated, is irresistibly reminded of the water front of Caernarfon, where the towers and gateway are still mirrored in the Menai Straits. And where else but in the Tour de Constance at Aigues Mortes can you find the model for the great Donjon at Flint - built at a time when such round keeps were already forty years out of fashion in Britain. Edward could never forget his continental experience.

But at Rhuddlan there was also something of a local prec-
edent-the Normans had not only built a motte-and-bailey
castle but had founded a defended borough with a church
and mint which in 1286 is recorded as having eighteen burgesses. Here Edward fostered the borough and endeavoured to
increase its prestige by trying to persuade Rome to let him
transfer the old Cathedral see of St. Asaph, a few miles away
in the valley of Clwyd, to the new town. He offered large
money inducements and a new cathedral as an added bait.
But Rome felt that this was going too far. St. Asaph's cathedral stayed where it still stands today.

So, around the shrunken borders of Llywelyn's principality Edward's new castles and towns steadily arose. This
first period of castle-building lasted for nearly six years
during which time the King of England might have hoped
that he had settled the Welsh problem. He had not treated the
Prince of Wales discourteously. He had waived some of the
harsher money terms of the Treaty of Aberconway. Llywelyn
had come to London and done homage, although his followers did not enjoy the curiosity of the Cockneys, who
crowded out to the Welsh lodgings at Islington to laugh at
the strange clothes and diet of the visitors. Edward himself
presided over Llywelyn's marriage to Eleanor de Montfort at
Worcester Cathedral, where Llywelyn, according to the
romantically inclined, even if celibate annalist of the Abbey
of Osney, gained "with a heart that lept for joy, his beloved
spouse, for whose loving embraces he had so long yearned."

There were other hearts in North Wales, however, that
were being stirred to quite different emotions. Llywelyn's
brother David resented what he regarded as the inadequate
provision made for him after the Treaty of Aberconway. He
had plenty of support from other Welshmen now placed for
the first time under complete English control. Edward may
have had no intention of being oppressive. Indeed what we
know of his character would indicate that he was anxious to
make a peaceful transition from the old regime to the new.
But his officials would obviously be more familiar with
English than with Welsh custom. Taxes which are collected

efficiently are never popular. Prominent Welshmen who had taken Edward's side in 1276 also began to regret the old days. All the materials for an explosion were steadily accumulating and in 1282 - six years after Edward's first Welsh war - that explosion occurred.

David seized the castle of Hawarden on Palm Sunday and soon the whole countryside was aflame. The royal castles at Aberystwyth, Llandovery and Carreg Cennen were attacked. The Welsh princes of South and West Wales joined in. And Llywelyn himself was inevitably forced to put himself at the head of the movement. Edward had to face the whole Welsh problem all over again. In 1282 he adopted exactly the same tactics for dealing with it that he had found so effective in 1276-7. And this time he had a splendid advanced base ready at Rhuddlan.

Once again he used his fleet to pen the Welsh forces into the wilds of Snowdonia while he cut them off from Anglesey. In vain the Welsh scored successes in Llandeilo Fawr where they defeated the Earl of Gloucester, and on the Menai Straits where they destroyed the bridge of boats built to get the English troops across onto the mainland. Llywelyn saw he would inevitably be starved out in his mountain stronghold if he did not create a powerful diversion elsewhere. He slipped over the hills and appeared in South Wales. By an unfortunate accident he became separated from his men near Builth. He was run through by an English knight near Cilmery, just outside Builth. His head was sent to Anglesey, where Edward exhibited it to his troops and then sent it for display in London. There was nothing particularly shocking to mediaeval minds in all this. The death of so prominent a leader had to be proved to the public. Lord Kitchener faced the same unpleasant duty when he dug up the head of the Mahdi after the capture of Omdurman! Llywelyn's body lies in the long-ruined abbey of Cwm Hir, where a thorn tree traditionally marks the site of the grave. A great slab of North Wales granite stands near the fatal spot at Cilmery.

With Llywelyn's death, the end of the second Welsh war was not long delayed. Edward captured Dolwyddelan castle in 1283, and David was betrayed into his hands. Edward had him painfully executed at Shrewsbury, and then faced the task of reorganising the whole extent of the land left by the two unfortunate princes. This he did on two fronts. He first made a political settlement embodied in the statute he issued at Rhuddlan in 1284. He took what was in effect Gwynedd and turned it into English shire ground. The counties of Anglesey, Caernarvonshire, Merioneth and Cardigan came into being, with part of Carmarthen. The germ of the present county of Flint was created. But clearly Edward did not have a free hand to re-cast the whole of Wales in a new mould. He had to reward his followers with lordships in Denbigh, Ruthin, Mold and Bromfield in North Wales. And over the rest of the country the great Marcher lordships remained intact. Wales had to wait until Henry VIII before it was completely tidied up administratively.

Edward, like all powerful rulers in the high Middle Ages, tried to symbolise his settlement by ceremonies and acts which he hoped would give sanction to the new regime. He had already caused the reputed grave of King Arthur and Queen Guinevere to be re-opened during his visit to Glastonbury in Easter, 1278, in the year following his first Welsh war. Adam of Dowerham, a monk of Glastonbury, was probably present and gives a vivid account of how the graves were opened at dusk and two caskets discovered, one of which contained the bones of the King, "of great size, and those of Queen Guinevere, which were of marvellous beauty". They were carefully reburied at the high altar, after the bones had been wrapped in precious silks. In all this, Edward was clearly symbolising his right to be the true ruler of an united Britain. He was reminding the world and the Welsh that Geoffrey of Monmouth had glorified Arthur as the only rightful King over the whole island. And here was Arthur himself buried with honour not on Welsh but English soil!

So, after the final overthrow of Llywelyn he held a great tournament at Nefyn, in North Wales, with ceremonial of an Arthurian splendour. His policy of embodying his power in

vivid symbols might also lend some truth to the most celebrated of the stories that have gathered around Edward's conquest of North Wales. It has now become firmly anchored to
Caernarfon castle and to the Investiture ceremony, but its
first appearance in literary form comes long after 1284 in a
history written in the sixteenth century. It is on a par with
the stories of the twelve Knights of Glamorgan and Prince
Madoc's reputed discovery of America in the 12th century -
the product of Tudor anxiety to glorify things Welsh in
honour of the Welsh dynasty on the throne.

Dr. David Powell relates in his History of Wales how, after
Edward had issued the Statute of Rhuddlan, the Welsh
nobles refused to obey any other "than a prince of their own
nation, of their own language, and whose life and conver-
sation was spotless and unblameable". Edward promised
them a prince who could not speak a word of English, who
was born in Wales and whose life was free from all stain. And
promptly named as Prince of Wales his infant son Edward,
who had recently been born in the castle of Caernarfon on
April 25, 1284. The King, however, was certainly at Rhuddlan at this time and the young prince Edward was brought
there on his way to England. He was not formally made
Prince of Wales until 1301, but it is possible that Dr. Powell's
story might have embodied an old tradition. Edward had
become heir to the throne in 1284 on the death of his eldest
brother Alphonso. Somehow it is hard to picture the Welsh
nobles enthusiastically hailing an Alphonso as Prince of
Wales!

Side by side with the political settlement came the military one. Edward began the second wave of his castle-
building in North Wales. His first series of castles had, as it
were, ringed the outer boundaries of the old Pura Wallia.
Now his task was to throw an iron ring around the inner core
of Gwynedd. He had to make certain that never again could
the Welsh link Anglesey with the mountains of Snowdonia
or use the Conway valley as a firm moat for this central
natural fortress.

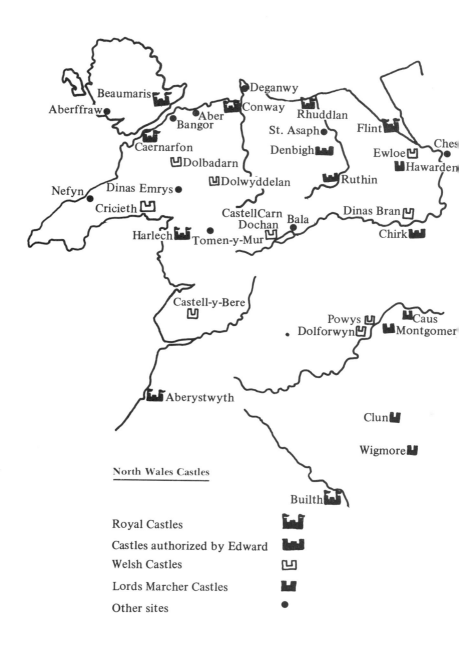

Beaumaris
Aberffraw
Deganwy
Conway
Aber
Bangor
Rhuddlan
St. Asaph
Flint
Caernarfon
Denbigh
Ewloe
Ches
Hawarden
Dolbadarn
Dolwyddelan
Ruthin
Nefyn
Dinas Emrys
Cricieth
CastellCarn
Dochan
Bala
Dinas Bran
Harlech
Tomen-y-Mur
Chirk

Castell-y-Bere

Powys
Caus
Dolforwyn
Montgomer

Clun

Wigmore

North Wales Castles

Aberystwyth

Builth

Royal Castles

Castles authorized by Edward

Welsh Castles

Lords Marcher Castles

Other sites

Three sites immediately commanded attention. A strong castle was essential to guard the vital crossing of the river Conway, and make certain that the difficult passage along the coast under the high mountains of the Carneddau was kept open. Then Anglesey had to be firmly cut off from the mainland. A further strong-point beyond the Snowdon range would separate the long peninsula of Lleyn from the inner fastness of Snowdon. So came into being that remarkable trio of castles that are such a spectacular attraction for the visitor to North Wales - Conway, Caernarfon, and Harlech.

Each one possesses its own individuality, but they also have certain things in common. They were all constructed under the general supervision of Master James and his team, and their construction involved a major feat of organisation. The team's experience in handling the construction, five years before, of Flint, Rhuddlan and Aberystwyth now stood them in good stead. Workmen and materials were gathered from all over England and moved swiftly to the building area. The time taken to begin the work was astonishingly short. For example, the Welsh castle of Dolwyddelan fell on January 18, 1283, and its fall opened up the Conway valley. Edward himself reached Conway around mid-March and within four days had issued the first orders for the construction of the new castle and town. The capture of the Castell y Bere near Towyn on April 25, 1283, cleared southern Gwynedd, while the last of the Welsh castles, Dolbadarn, fell by May. Work was already in progress at Caernarfon and Harlech by mid-summer, hardly a few weeks after the collapse of Welsh resistance.

Each building project was conceived on the same principle - the castle and the new town were regarded as a single unit and their construction proceeded simultaneously, the first urgent need being to throw up some sort of circuit capable of defence. In Harlech the town defences, if any, would have been earthen banks and palisades as at Rhuddlan and Flint. Conway and Caernarfon castles and towns were always regarded by Edward as something special and were conceived as stone constructions on a grander scale. But town and castle still grew together. The first workmen on the scene would be the ditch-diggers and the masons who would rush up the defensive lines. The craftsmen would come a little later. The major costs of every project would have to be incurred in the first few years. The enormous financial strain put on the royal finances can well be imagined. By 1292 about £12,000 had been spent on the town and castle of Caernarfon - equivalent in our money today at at least £3,000,000. Conway had absorbed £15,000, say £4,000,000 at the present time. Harlech was going forward on a similar scale. Other new works, at places like Aberystwyth and Builth were still costing Edward big money, while the defences of the former Welsh castles at Dolwyddelan, Cricieth and Castell y Bere were also being strengthened at the King's expense. No wonder that by 1296 the King faced a major financial crisis, which brought bankruptcy to some of his Italian bankers. The Welsh were not the only ones who looked on the royal castle-building with a jaundiced eye!

As today, wages took up a great percentage of the cash available. The work force was raised in England and was distributed among the castles as the work required. The records show in interesting detail where some of the workmen came from, and what the estimates were for the raw materials. We read, for example, of 20 carpenters who were recruited from Northamptonshire; of a 70-strong contingent of labourers who assembled at Newport Pagnell and set off on their long journey to the west with a little cart to carry their tools. There were masons who travelled the whole way from Yorkshire. Edward poured out his orders to the royal officials in the counties of England to speed the workmen on their way. Many of them were recruited under pressure and must have had a shock when they saw the wild, rainy hills of Wales!

We also know the names of the higher echelons of the master-craftsmen. Many of them came from abroad but some had solid English names like Master Philip of Pasley, Master Richard of Chester and Master Lawrence of Canterbury. Not a Welshman amongst them, naturally, even Edward would not have invited the Welsh to plan their own prison walls! Among the masons we find John of Sherwood, Roger of Cockersand and Robert of Frankby. Like any group of men engaged on a big construction project today, they were constantly running into difficulties. They may have written to each other in far more courtly style, and ended their letters with "Farewell forever in the Lord" instead of "Yours faithfully", but they still wanted their materials on the spot quicker than those lazy blighters at base could supply. I wonder how long those 120,000 nails took to reach Conway which were ordered from Newcastle at 7d. per thousand inclusive of carriage. Or whether the 500 lbs of tin were satisfactory? And was the price of £3.11.4. considered extravagant?

Much of the material would have come by sea, for these new northern castles possessed another important common factor - they were all placed on sites next to the sea. Edward knew the value of sea power. The castles might get surrounded and cut off on the land side, but as long as the Welsh had no fleet, these new strong points could always be reinforced from the sea.

Caernarfon and Conway are without doubt the most splendid of Edward's castles, and they differ from the others in ways that clearly show that the King had a special role for them in mind. To begin with, they are not concentric, although perhaps too much weight must not be given to this. Master James, in both cases, was dealing with narrow rocky sites which did not allow room for deployment and which possessed great natural defensive power. Both are linked closely to a magnificent circuit of stone town-walls which form added defences in themselves; and both possess architectural features which are over and above those needed for mere defence.

Conway may have been originally intended to be the centre of the new county Edward proposed to carve out of this part of Gwynedd. It was to have royal apartments worthy of its position. Edward moved part of the old monastery of Aberconway to a new site up river to make room for a royal "bastide" on a really big scale. The castle itself, although it looks such a superbly homogeneous mass from without, is really divided into two sections. The Outer Ward faces the town side and contains the accommodation for the constable of the castle and his garrison. The strength of the garrison, in 1283, was set at 30 men. There were 15 cross-bowmen, and a similar number of watchmen and castle servants. In addition, there would be a chaplain, a smith, a mason, a carpenter and an armourer. The number does not seem large, but the whole purpose of a well-designed castle was to create a fortress that could be held by comparatively few defenders. The garrison could be reinforced in times of trouble.

The Inner Ward was completely independent of the Outer and had its separate barbican and a postern gate going down to the water's edge. It was designed to be approached from the Conway estuary and contained halls and apartments on a royal scale. Clearly this section of the castle was planned for the King's own use, and for his especial safety. The tower of the Inner Ward was fitted with extra, slender turrets from which the royal banners would fly when the King was in residence. Banners in the Middle Ages were not just pleasant decorations. They were visible and important indications of power. Men were prepared to spend money on them. At Rhuddlan, Adam the Tailor was paid 64 shillings for four pieces of red silk to make pennons and royal standards to fly from the castle turrets.

Caernarfon was also designed, like Conway, to impress as well as to defend. It was marked out for a splendid future from the moment of its inception. Here would live the Justiciar for the whole of North Wales and Edward appointed one of his closest collaborators, Sir Otto de Grandson, to the position. But he looked beyond the immediate future to the day when his eldest son would preside over the principality of Wales. Caernarfon should be both castle and residence. Here at Caernarfon, where memory of the Romans was still vivid and where it was firmly though mistakenly believed that the father of the great Emperor Constantine was buried, Edward planned his new castle to echo the old imperial glories. The remarkable multi-angular towers and the layers of different-hued stonework may well have been inspired by the walls of Byzantium and the great Byzantine palaces. On the highest and noblest of the towers Edward set the old image of Roman imperial power, the eagle. The two great gateways are exceptionally powerful. The King's Gate towers over the town and is the strongest gateway in all the castles of Wales. The Queen's Gate, which allowed access to the castle independently of the circuit of the town walls, was likewise fitted with a massive turning bridge. The ditch was dug on a formidable scale by hundreds of "fossatores" who began work immediately under Master Manasser from Vaucoleurs in Champagne. Like many of the foreign overseers he eventually settled in Wales and held municipal office in the Caernarfon he had helped to build.

At the same time that Caernarfon was rising along the banks of the river Seiont, work was being driven forward at Harlech. The site is magnificent, perched on a crag that faces Snowdonia and which, in those days, rose directly from the sea. A strong postern gate on the sea-edge allowed the castle to bring in its sea-borne supplies which would be carried up a heavily protected flight of stairs, along the crag into the Outer Ward. In the Inner Ward, the gatehouse dominates everything. It was designed not only as the residence of the castellian but as an independent defence point which could hold out even if the rest of the castle was over-run. But this is no old-fashioned keep, skulking as it were in the background of the defence. The keep at Harlech is defiant and aggressive. It would stand in the forefront of the battle.

At this same time, work was in hand at Cricieth, where Edward's architect took the old Welsh castle as the outer ring and planted a second ring within it, complete with the standard gatehouse and its two powerful flanking towers. Thus while Harlech was a concentric castle from the start, Cricieth was so modified as to become one.

Caernarfon, Harlech and Cricieth were to need their new strength, as indeed did the rest of Edward's new castles. The death of Llywelyn and David did not mean that all Wales was quiescent and peaceful. Some Welshmen, especially the official class trained in administration under the two Llywelyns, transferred their loyalties to the new men in power with the speed and ease of modern, top civil servants. Others resented the whole new, unsympathetic English regime. There was a series of rebellions culminating in a major uprising under Madog ap Llywelyn in 1294. The attackers swarmed around Edward's castles and even pursued the King into Conway, where he had ample opportunities of seeing for himself the defensive strength of this particular link in his Iron Ring. Harlech held as well, but Caernarfon fell - its main defensive circuit had not yet been completed.

The revolt had shown Edward one thing clearly: his Iron Ring of castles needed further strengthening. A new link was essential at the north end of the Menai Straits. So began, what we might call, the third phase of Edwardian castle-building. At Beaumaris Master James of St. George immediately started to build what must surely be the perfect concentric castle. The site was flat and on the coast. There were no rocks, streams or previous castle-buildings on the ground, and thus there were no obstructions to the development of the ideal concentric plan.

Beaumaris shows the same mathematic pleasure in its layout as the plans of Rhuddlan and, indeed, of Harlech. All is utterly logical. First comes the moat. Then the outer defensive circuit, guarded at regular intervals by round towers. Then the inner circuit, overlapping the outer one to give it extra fire support and containing the administrative heart of the castle. The strong gatehouse of the outer circuit is completed by a barbican defending the passage over the moat, and a fortified dock that could take ships up to 40 tons burden. From the air, Beaumaris has a splendid beauty of design.

To this third phase of castle-building we should add the work now pushed forward at three other points which were not precisely under Edward's direct control. As part of the political settlement of 1284, the King had felt it incumbent on him to reward certain of his supporters. Lordships were

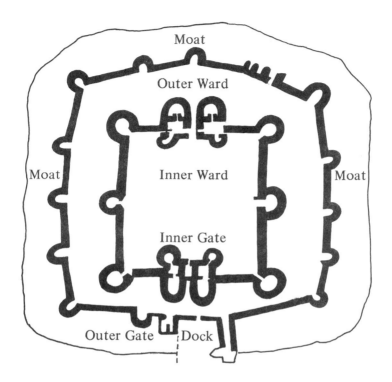

Beaumaris

granted at Denbigh to Henry de Lacy, Earl of Lincoln, and at Chirk to the old Marcher family of the Mortimers. These men were charged to build castles which could be regarded as supplementing the ones being built by the King himself. The work started in 1282 but it received a new impetus after Madog's revolt. The barons adopted the same principle as their King; town walls went forward side by side with those of the castles. We can also detect the controlling hand of Master James of St. George - certainly at Denbigh.

Here the great gateway and the two nearest towers are multi-angular, reminiscent of Caernarfon, and it is no surprise to find that de Lacy had close family connections with the House of Savoy.

Master James. no doubt, was happy to repeat at Denbigh

his successes at Caernarfon and St. Georges.

To those two castles should be added that at Ruthin, begun in 1277 as a royal castle, but handed over for completion to Reginald de Grey.

This third phase, as it were, of Edward's castle building was not without influence even on castle-building in South Wales, since in practice the elimination of Gwynedd did not prove to have removed all need for strengthening the existing castles. Caerphilly was to be put to its first serious test during the fierce revolt of Llywelyn Bren in 1316. The castle was lightly manned yet was able to hold out against the assailants. But the rebellion had shown that all South Wales castle-owners still had need to keep strengthening their defences. At St. Donat's on the coast of Glamorgan, the Stradling family built a small concentric castle. Further west, Kidwelly, which already possessed an inner circuit of stone, now replaced the outer earthen rampart with a magnificent ring of stone towers. After Caerphilly, Kidwelly is the finest concentric castle in South Wales.

Caerphilly came once more onto the stage of history in the tragic closing year of the reign of Edward II. Edward has received a bad press. The son of Edward I has been depicted as a vacillating homosexual who led England to disaster in Scotland and outraged the baronage at home. Some modern historians are inclined to take a more lenient view. One thing is certain. He had the sympathy of a great number of Welshmen. They accepted and supported the first English Prince of Wales with an enthusiasm they never showed to his successors. They stood by him even in his collapse, and it is significant that it was to South Wales that the unhappy Edward fled when his estranged wife Isabella landed in East Anglia with her paramour, Mortimer, to eliminate the influence of the hated favourites, the Despensers. The whole lurid tragedy was closely linked with the politics of the Welsh Marches. Roger Mortimer was at the Queen's side, as lover and leader of the rebellious barons. The King's favourite, the younger Despenser, had married Eleanor, who had inherited the vast de Clare estates in Glamorgan when her brother

Gilbert had been slain at Bannockburn. Two great Marcher lords were once again clashing in deadly rivalry that was affecting the whole political structure of England. When all support fell away from them, Edward and the young Despenser naturally fled westwards into South Wales and Caerphilly, taking with them the royal treasure and personal records. After some anguished wandering through Glamorgan, Edward and Despenser were captured near Llantrisant, maybe in a dingle that tradition still names as Pant-y-Brad — the Vale of Treachery. Edward was taken back into England to his eventual shameful death at Berkeley castle. Caerphilly was closely besieged and finally surrendered on the promise of favourable terms.

There followed a grand treasure hunt which, in some ways, continued up to our own times. Edward had scattered his wealth for safe keeping not only in Caerphilly castle, but at castles and monasteries further west - at Margam, Neath and Swansea amongst other places. The royal commissioners who hunted for the royal money-chest, armour and valuable documents were still hard at it years after the fall of Edward II. Who knows if some of his money may not still turn up in unexpected places in our own day? A workman recently picked up a fine gold brooch of the period in Oxwich castle. It might have been part of a horde which Robert de Penres, Lord of Penrice, was suspected of illegally removing in 1331. Again, a small horde of coins was uncovered a few years back during restoration work in Neath Abbey. But the strangest find of all occurred in the middle of the last century. Dr. Nichol of Swansea was called to a case in a remote part of Gower. In payment for his service, the farmer offered him a box which he withdrew from a hiding place in the thatched roof. The box contained the parchment of the original document recording Edward II's affiancement to his queen Isabella. It is now preserved in the Royal Institution of Swansea.

The end of Edward II also marked the end of Caerphilly's role in history. From then on, the greatest castle in Wales went back onto the sidelines. It had outlived the purpose for which it was built. At the very period when Caerphilly was under siege by the forces of Mortimer and Isabella, we find the first mention of a new invention which would eventually eclipse, not only Caerphilly, but all the other splendid 13th century castles as well. Around 1325, gunpowder appears on the European battle scene. For the men behind the battlements in the mediaeval castle, the sound of gunpowder was the sound of doom.

7

The Sound of Doom

No one knows who actually invented the revolutionary mixture of sulphur, saltpetre and charcoal which was eventually to change the history of the whole world. Modern historians will have nothing to do with Black Berthold, the Monk of Freiburg who was supposed to have discovered gunpowder somewhere around 1313 and then applied it for use in a gun. In fact they doubt if this ingenious monk ever existed. Gunpowder may have come from the Far East, since saltpetre was called "Chinese snow" in Egypt in 1248. Or it might have been developed quite naturally from the researches of technicians in Europe itself. Roger Bacon, around 1250, seems to have been aware of its explosive power. It is certain however that guns were already on the military scene by 1326. In that year the artist illuminating a manuscript of Walter de Millemete, now preserved in the library of Christ Church, Oxford, depicted a large bottle shaped affair with an arrow inserted in the mouth, being fired by a soldier who had every excuse for looking nervous. The gun arrived not with a bang but a whimper.

Guns soon became more elaborate. The earliest examples which have survived, including the one fished out of the sands of Morecambe Bay and the great gun called Mons Meg at Edinburgh Castle, were made of wrought iron rods. The rods were bound together by red hot iron rings which were shrunk onto the rods to hold them in a vice-like grip. Lead would then be poured into the interstices and the whole barrel carefully smoothed. Later on improvements in the techniques of handling metal allowed guns to be made of cast iron. These early guns were dragged on sledges or placed on elaborate stands. They grew steadily in size and power during the 14th and 15th centuries.

The gunpowder they employed was almost as dangerous to the gunner as to the enemy, and was sometimes mixed on the actual battlefield - a very perilous performance indeed. No wonder the master gunner was known as the "Artist". All gunners were experts set apart from the ordinary soldiers and practising a mystery dedicated to St. Barbara, the patron saint of artillery men. Gunpowder became more reliable with the invention of the process known as "corning" or the shaping of the powder into standard sized grains. Some experts recommended using alcohol and urine to stabilize the mixture and suggested that an incontinent wine drinker should always be attached to the gun team!

Guns were expensive items and the King was the only man who could afford to set up a factory for making them on anything like a large scale. Under Edward III the Tower of London became the Royal arsenal. England, however, was never in the lead in the business of making these early guns. Many of them were purchased on the continent, and it wasn't until the reign of Henry VIII that gun making was placed on a proper footing in this country.

The early guns were essentially siege weapons. The effective use of artillery in the field was very much a later development. In the beautifully illuminated manuscripts of the 14th and 15th centuries guns became favourite objects for the artists. They are shown shielded by heavy screens, battering away at the curtain walls of the castles. Some guns were double-barrelled, others elegantly decorated, but all were christened with a splendidly varied collection of names. We hear of the big guns, or bombards called Cannons Royal or carthouns, of culverins and demi-culverins, of sakers and dragons and of smaller pieces like falconets, robinets and aspics. But impressive as they sound, none were big enough to put the castle immediately out of business. It was to take centuries of steadily developing techniques before the gun made the mediaeval type of fortification completely obsolete. The thick walls of a Conway or Harlech would take a lot of battering before they were breached. Thus, even in the Civil War, the castles of Wales still had an important part to play, even though they now existed under the continued threat of the gun.

The great period of castle building in Wales, however, was over by the time the gun began to be a decisive factor in siege warfare. The end of independent Gwynedd had removed the need for new castle construction on the heroic scale of Edward I. All the essential strategic sites were now provided with fortifications. These fortifications were being continually elaborated and improved throughout the 14th century. The great gatehouse of Kidwelly, for example, belongs to this period but completely new castles are rare. The political scene in the hundred years that followed the final settlement of Gwynedd by Edward did not demand them.

The 14th century is a curiously puzzling one in Welsh History. The late Professor Glyn Roberts called it the century of antipathy and sympathy. The antipathy to all the new alien English administration was obviously present as a steady undercurrent in the national life. The new townsfolk were still suspicious of their Welsh neighbours. Town walls continue to be kept in constant repair. But there was sympathy too. The high placed men just below the princely clan could see opportunities in the new situation. By the end of the 14th century they were getting a grip once again on local administration. The fighting men could enter the service of the crown with hope of a successful career, for under Edward III the Hundred Years War with France had begun. Welsh long-bowmen were in demand, and played a major part in the victory of Creçy. When the Black Prince was thrown from his horse, the banner of the Red Dragon of Wales was thrown around him for protection. According to tradition it was at Creçy that the Welshmen picked leeks as they went into battle and wore them in their hats to distinguish themselves from their enemies. The leek, and after the leek its more polite version the daffodil, thus became the national emblem of Wales.

A whole host of Welshmen made their name and money on the battlefields of France. Some of them even penetrated into the inner bastion of English power, the constableship of a royal castle. Around 1359 that celebrated soldier the genial Sir Hywel ap Gruffydd, returned with honour from the French wars, and became constable of Cricieth. The bards hastened to sing his praises. To them he was Sir Hywel y Fywall, "Sir Howell of the Battle Axe", from the weapon which had won him glory in his French campaigns. For years after his death, it was placed before the great dish of meat served annually to the poor in his memory. His long term as constable was remembered as a golden age in Cricieth. A little later there were Welsh under-constables in this castle including one with the delightful name of Jevan ap Willie Boy.

But behind the seeming acquiescence to English rule there were deep forces stirring which were to lead to the furious outbreak of the revolt of Owain Glyn Dŵr. Owain Glyn Dŵr, Shakespeare's Owen Glendower, is still a magic name in Wales. He was the last of the great men who had a chance to create an independent principality. There is still something mysterious about his rising and its staggering initial success. Owain came from that very clan of "Uchelwyr" who had made their peace with the English settlement and done very well out of the process.

He had studied at the Inns of Court. He had served the crown against the Scots in 1385 and had won golden opinions for his personal bravery. He had an income of £200 a year which made him a rich man by mediaeval standards. The bards praised the open hearted hospitality he dispensed at his seat at Sycharth, girdled by its moat of shining water and its finely carved wooden hall on the hilltop. The great mound of Sycharth is still there but Owain's hall and all its outbuildings have disappeared, burnt in the great revolt he inspired.

The causes of that revolt are still obscure. The Marches of Wales had suffered from the same social troubles that followed the Black Death in England. There were new men forcing their way to the front, heavier burdens laid upon the peasantry, and always in the background the siren voices of the bards hinting that all would be well if only the country would return to the old ways of independent Wales. Owain was borne along by irresistible pressure. What began as a typical marcher quarrel over a piece of land with his neighbour, Lord Grey of Ruthin, turned into a national revolt. Once again, England's difficulty was Wales's opportunity. Henry IV had violently deposed Richard II and seized the crown. The King was now in the toils of baronial troubles on a big scale. He would not have the money, the time, and the resources to mount a major assault on the Welsh rebels. The revolt prospered and the key to its success was the fall of many of the great castles.

Owain did not at first possess a siege train but he got temporary possession of the seemingly impregnable castle of Conway by a ruse. His men rushed in when the fortress was carelessly guarded and the garrison were all at Church! Caernarfon held out against him although the town fell, and Harlech surrendered after long sieges. Their garrisons were small - Cricieth was defended by a man-at-arms and twelve bowmen. Reinforcements were authorised too late. Owain had received the help of a Breton and French fleet and the garrisons were thus placed in the classic position of having no hope of relief. Aberystwyth went the same way. Cricieth was heavily damaged by Owain and never again recovered its importance. But Harlech and Aberystwyth were retained as firm bases for the rebellion and a symbol of Owain's success. The castle still represented power and governing authority.

When the revolt spread through South Wales, castles fell like ninepins mainly through collusion. Glyn Dŵr had secret supporters everywhere. Cardiff went and even Carreg Cennen. Coity sent out desperate appeals for rescue to Henry IV. In the high tide of success Owain Glyn Dŵr seemed irresistib.e, allied to the French, holding parliaments at Machynlleth and planning an independent church and two universities for Wales.

It could not last. As Henry IV got the better of his enemies he was able to support his son, Prince Henry, with more soldiers and above all with money. Owain's French support fell away. Prince Henry closed in. In 1408 he was able to march onto Owain's main bases at Aberystwyth and Harlech. It was now that guns proved their worth. Owain had always been short of artillery, but Prince Henry could call on the Royal arsenal. The great guns were shipped down from Yorkshire where they were no longer needed against the Northern Barons. They were transhipped at Bristol and then brought by sea to the Cardigan coast. Stone shot, sulphur and saltpetre were gathered in quantities at the base of Hereford. The fortresses did not fall at the first shot. Aberystwyth held out for a long time but the guns made the end inevitable. It was the same with Harlech. Some of the great stone cannon balls that were fired from the bombards of the besiegers are still there, one of them 22″ in diameter, which is big by any standards. Owain's wife, daughter and grandchildren were captured at Harlech, and although the old hero went on the run and was never taken, the loss of the castles meant a fatal loss of prestige. The end of the rebellion was only a matter of time.

Owain's revolt left an appalling legacy of destruction and misery behind it. Hatred sprang anew between the Welsh and the English. As late as 1436 the authors of "The Libell of English Policye" could still write:

> "Beware of Wales; Christ Jesu must us keep
> That it makes not our child's child to weep."

The poets such as Lewis Glyn Cothi were equally bitter on the Welsh side. Yet Welshmen were aware that Owain had altered the course of their history. Welsh nationality, it is said, really begins in 1410.

A large bill had to be paid for the repair of the castles. Cricieth was permanently ruined and Carreg Cennen had to be restored at great cost. The report talks of urgent repairs to the walls lately completely destroyed and thrown down by the rebels. The repairs to the great gatehouse at Kidwelly cost £500. And so it goes on. But it is clear that in spite of the power of the guns, castle owners still felt that it was worth while restoring damage and keeping their castles in repair, especially in the middle of the 15th century when the shadow of those unhappy civil wars, the Wars of the Roses, began to lengthen over the land. Henry V had won glory at Agincourt and there were plenty of Welshmen there to support him, from the indispensible long bow-men of Gwent to fiery warriors like Sir David Gam. But as the French Wars turned sour, the old soldiers returned and not always with loot. The times were turning dangerous for the smaller men. Their open manor houses would be all the better for a little fortification. At Tretower the Vaughan family built their house in a square with a tower over the gateway and all windows looking inwards to a central courtyard. At Llantilio Crossenny in Monmouthshire a deep moat surrounds the Hen Gwrt, the Old Court, which tradition associates with Sir David Gam who died at Agincourt. But the great show place, the finest example in Wales of the castle striving to adapt itself to the new conditions created by guns and the threat of civil war, is Raglan.

Again the builder was a warrior who had come back with money from the French Wars and set about fishing for an even greater fortune and estate in the troubled waters at home. Sir William ap Thomas had won fame as the Blue Knight of Gwent. He needed a castle not only for the safe keeping of his wealth but as a symbol of his social success. Raglan was to be a flamboyant gesture of power to the surrounding countryside. It would be what was then termed a "castle of livery and maintenance" - that is, one manned by professional soldiers who were paid and maintained to wear the livery of their lord. But such men were dangerous. A lord who relied totally on purchased loyalty could never feel completely safe in his castle unless he had a special section of it designed as a sure retreat, cut off from the rest of the building. The solution adopted was to revive the idea of the Keep. Hence that remarkable structure at Raglan known as the Yellow Tower of Gwent. This nobly built tower was surrounded by a deep wet moat, and provided with two separate drawbridges. There were also loop holes for small guns. Here Sir William could beat a quick retreat and keep his valuables in what was in effect a gigantic stone safe. His son, Sir William Herbert, continued the building of the rest of the castle in the same splendid style. His great gatehouse contains the finest examples of machicolations in stone in Britain. Provision was also made for small gun ports all through the defensive circuit.

No one can say how long Raglan could have stood up to a really serious bombardment by the guns of the period; to the sort of treatment for example that Henry V gave Harfleur in the Agincourt campaign, where the great bombard known as the King's Daughter battered away remorselessly at the town wall until a breach was made and the town surrendered. Given time the gun was bound to win, as it did at Raglan in the Civil War. It is difficult to believe, however, that the small gun ports built into the walls at Raglan could have offered a really effective reply to the giant bombards and carthoons, even in the fifteenth century. The castle had to be far more drastically reconstructed if it was to keep pace with the development of the gun. It had to turn itself into a series of gun platforms, and in doing so it ceased to be the castle whose fortunes we have been following through the Middle Ages. In fact it was no longer a castle but a fort.

Technical reasons were not the only cause of this profound change in the destiny of the castle. There were political reasons as well. Raglan was the last attempt in Wales to build a castle in the mediaeval style - a fortress that was not only a strong defensive structure but was also the home of a ruler and the centre of administration. The Wars of the Roses were the swan song of the Marcher Lords. They committed suicide as a clan in the treacherously shifting alliances, blood feuds, pointless battles and betrayals that made up the history of Wales as well as England for twenty years. At last the deliverer came who put an end to the social and political chaos. The Welsh were proud to point out that he came from Wales in the person of Henry Tudor, Henry VII.

The Tudors were not a princely family in origin. They sprang from Ednyfed Fechan, who was the seneschal of Llywelyn the Great. The family fortunes were made by Owen Tudor in the days that followed the death of Henry V. Never was sexual attraction more potent in the history of Britain. This young Welshman of no great fortune was on the spot when Henry V died early, leaving his young widow, Katherine of France, beautiful and clearly in need of romance. Katherine was bowled over and gave the handsome Owen two sons, Edmund and Jasper. Edmund married Margaret Beaufort, who was a descendant of John of Gaunt. Their son was Henry Tudor, the future Henry VII. His claim to the throne was thus extremely tenuous and it would never have had a chance if the slaughter of the Wars of the Roses hadn't destroyed many of the better claimants. Owen Tudor himself was executed. He laid down his head on the block with a word to the executioner to be careful of "a head that was wont to lie in a queen's lap". The young Henry, who had been born in Pembroke castle, was smuggled off to Britanny for safety. The Tudors were Lancastrian supporters and shared in the ruin of that cause after the Yorkist triumph of 1468. Harlech castle was the last Lancastrian stronghold to surrender. Its defender was a stout veteran of the French wars, Dafydd ap Enion. He had made the memorable boast: "I kept a castle in France for so long that all the old women in Wales heard about it. Now I will keep a castle in Wales so long that all the old French women will hear about it". He surrendered it, nevertheless. The March of The Men of Harlech is a stirring latter-day reminder of those times. Needless to say, it contains no mention of the castle's surrender.

Castles on the whole did not feature very prominently in the Wars of the Roses. The issue was decided by pitched battles in the field. The gun had already made the castle walls unsafe. Their fate was finally sealed when Henry Tudor landed at Dale on Milford Haven and began his celebrated march through Wales to Bosworth Field. The Welsh flocked to his standard, including the all-powerful magnate of South Wales, Sir Rhys ap Thomas. As Henry led his supporters up the west coast, David Lloyd, the bard and prophet, was waiting for him near Machynlleth, and prudently prophesied victory on his wife's shrewd advice: "If he wins he'll never forget you. If he loses you can forget him." Henry won, and Wales, and England too, did not forget.

The age of the Tudors began. Here was a line of successful rulers who had no use for the over-powerful subject in his proud castle. There were to be no more private wars, or private justice. Under Henry VIII the whole complicated structure of the rule of the Lords Marcher was swept away. Two comprehensive acts united Wales with England. The gentry of Wales accepted the Tudor settlement with alacrity. They willingly became Tudor Justices of the Peace, although, as one Welsh historian remarked, many of them neither administered justice or kept the peace! There was no necessity for castle building of any sort. The king held all the great guns in his Royal arsenal in the Tower. If there was any need for fortifications, he would build them.

Henry VIII did, in fact, construct a series of forts along the South coast of England but none in Wales. At Walmer or Pendennis in Cornwall you can see how completely different the new type constructions are from the old mediaeval castle. They are elaborate gun platforms with immensely thick walls, and with accommodation within for gunners and their ammunition. They have no Great Hall, no apartments for the Lord and his family, no stables for the horses, no chapel for the resident priest. They are straightforward fighting positions designed to be manned by a royal army and not by the retainers of a great lordl. The age of the castle had ended. The age of the fort begins.

What, then, was to be done with the castles which had now become obsolete. Some were deliberately let fall into decay. Part of Carreg Cennen was actually torn down during the Wars of the Roses by a force of 500 men at a cost of £28. 5. 6. "foreasmuch as all the misgoverned men of the country there intended to have inhabited the castle and to have lived by robbery and spoiling of our people". The great gateway at Llanstephan was blocked up and it ultimately sank into the obscurity of a mere farm building. The Royal castles in North Wales still had some sort of function to perform. They were depots for arms, the seat of local courts and, as at Harlech, the residence of Judge on circuit. But the Crown became increasingly reluctant to spend money on them. By the end of the Tudor period the castle of Conway was in a sad state "the leads being decayed and broken above, and almost all the floors fallen down". Many of the Marcher castles were equally forlorn.

The walls of the major castles, however, were usually left intact, with important results a hundred and fifty years later. Castles were built to last. Even if there did not seem to be a use for them, they remained obstinately upright. The Tudor period created an aristocracy of new men, pledged to the support of the crown. Many of them felt the need to buttress their newly acquired honours with the glory of the past. It does not pay to look too closely into the pedigrees of the great names at the Courts of the Tudors, but certain ancient castles were remodelled to provide a convincing background to the men of power, favoured by Henry VIII and Elizabeth. Thus Chirk became the seat of the Middletons and Powys remained a residence of a great family. Picton Castle in Pembrokeshire, though it has been extensively remodelled through the ages, remained a family seat and makes the proud claim to be the oldest continually inhabited castle in the British Isles.

Once again Raglan is the classic example of this form of Tudor development. The Herberts, the descendants of Sir Rhys ap Thomas, remodelled the 15th century castle to 16th century standards. The Third Earl of Worcester (for the Herberts had risen high and fast) rebuilt the Fountain Court and the Pitched Stone Court - a great gallery ran between them. This was a major reconstruction in characteristic Renaissance style. Raglan shows exactly what a great Tudor magnate wanted to keep from the past to help him shine in the

future. Thomas Churchyard, The Elizabethan poet-
traveller saw the castle in 1587 and celebrated its glories:

Not far from thence, a famous castle fine
That Raggland height, stands moted almost round:
Made of freestone, upright as straight as line,
Whole workmanship in beauty doth abound.
The curious knots, wrought all with edged tool,
The stately tower, that looks o'er pond and pool:
The fountain trim, that runs both day and night,
Doth yield in show a rare and noble sight.

Raglan was finally overthrown in the Civil Wars, but even
today the ruins have a moving splendour. As in an Oxford
college, one quadrangle leads into another. The great hall is
the centre of its social life, maintaining a tradition inherited
from the old mediaeval castles. The solar had now developed into a multiplicity of noble apartments. Above all the
blank walls of the castle were pierced with elegant windows.
A gentleman had no need to live crouched behind the safety
of high defences. The Tudors had brought peace to the
countryside. Even the minor nobles could afford to build elegant houses with no serious defensive purpose behind them.
The Bassetts of Beaupré in the Vale of Glamorgan, not far
from Cardiff, constructed a splendid manor house with a
porch in the inner courtyard of full Renaissance glory, complete with classical columns. We have come a long way from
the stark grim windowless strength of the 11th and 12th
century keeps at Chepstow and Ogmore. Carew castle, on the
upper reaches of Milford Haven, is another splendid example of the way Tudor castle owners tried to open up their
grim fortresses to the new, safer and exciting world outside.
In the days of Henry VII it belonged to the greatest of his
Welsh supporters, Sir Rhys ap Thomas. He reconstructed
the great hall, and brought a new lightness to the inner
courtyard. Under Elizabeth, Sir John Perrot opened up the
North front with a series of beautiful mullioned windows.

Carew was changed from a powerful, enceinte type 13th century castle into a light airy palace which would not have been out of place among the Chateaux of the Loire.

It was here that Sir Rhys ap Thomas celebrated his elevation to the honour of the Garter in 1507 with a great tournament to which he invited all the leading men in Wales. It was the last tournament on the old lavish scale to be held in Britain and lasted for five days. The great men were quartered in the castle while their retainers lived in a forest of brightly coloured tents outside. There was high feasting in the great hall. The bards sang the praises of Sir Rhys in ecstatic verse. Two hundred retainers in blue livery formed a guard of honour through which the champions passed down to the lists. Sir Rhys, clad in gilded armour, sat in the judges' chair. The heirs to the new Tudor nobility - Herberts, Salisbury's, Mansells and Vaughans - broke their lances at the tilt. Hunting, more feasting and the acting of a comedy. "St. George's pilgrimage to St. David's" filled in the rest of the crowded days. And when the guests at last departed, it was noted as a marvel that "although one thousand men had spent five days in company, not one quarrel, unkind word or cross look had passed between them". The great tournament of Carew cast a last, sunset glow over the fading power and splendour of the castle of the Middle Ages.

8
Swan Song

Through the long Tudor peace the castles of Wales began their slow decline into obscurity. There were exceptions like Carew and Raglan, which had been given a face-lift by their owners to suit them to their new role in society. But travellers reported that numbers of the Welsh castles were "marvellously decayed". No one expected that they would ever go to war again. Wales had been firmly united to England under a dynasty of impeccably Welsh origins. The new nobility was steadily anglicising itself. Squire William Vaughan of Llangyndeyrn could declare with confidence, "I rejoice that the memorial of Offa's Ditch is extinguished with love and charity; that our green leeks, somewhat offensive to your dainty nostrils, are now tempered with your fragrant roses . . . God give us to dwell together for eternity, without detraction". Later generations of Welshmen might take a different and less rose-coloured view of the Tudor settlement, but at the time all seemed well and fair. When the Tudor dynasty ended, the majority of Welshmen of property and position felt no difficulty in transferring their loyalty to the Stuarts. Welsh and English politics were now inextricably intermingled. Wales, therefore, shared completely in the anguish of the Civil Wars of the 17th century.

The great explosive forces that impelled the Parliamentary party to rebellion had no strong roots in Wales. The merchant classes which supplied the sinews of war for

Parliament were weak in the Principality. Country Wales became "the nursery of the King's infantry". There were, however, certain Parliamentary islands in the middle of the general sea of loyalty. In the north, Sir Thomas Myddleton held the Chirk area for Parliament. In the south west, the English-speaking areas were on the whole strongly against the King. The Earl of Pembroke, with his great influence in the Vale of Glamorgan, was also anti-royalist. As the rival parties took up positions for the struggle, they looked around for bases on which to form their forces. The only real strong-points available were the old castles.

They were hopelessly out-of-date by continental standards. The constant warfare in Europe had led to notable advances in the art of fortification. The individual castle may have ceased to be of importance, as in Britain, but European towns and vital strategic centres had been surrounded with elaborate defensive works, designed to take full advantage of the growing power of the gun. In the reign of Louis XIV this process reached a splendid climax with the work of the great military engineer, Vauban, who protected the eastern frontiers of France with forts and fortified towns which still astonish the modern expert. A fortification like Neuf Breisach in Alsace, for example, has the same formal mathematical beauty that Master James of St. George gave to Beaumaris three centuries earlier.

With the possible exception of Berwick-on-Tweed, and a few castles like Carisbrooke in the Isle of Wight, fortification on this scale did not exist in Britain. The forts built by Henry VIII could not compare with the great defensive structures which now surrounded the cities of Northern France, Germany and the Low Countries. But the rival forces had no option. They had to do the best they could with the old castles. No one expected them to hold out against a major assault backed by big guns, but they could still hold off sudden attacks by lightly armed forces. In some cases, it might be possible to supplement the old walls with earthworks more suited to modern warfare. The Parliamentarians therefore hastened to garrison Pembroke,

Cardiff, and some of the border castles in North Wales. The
royalists occupied Chepstow in the south, and most of the
Edwardian castles in the north. Conway was specially important since it protected the route to Ireland, from which
the King hoped to draw men and supplies. Archbishop
Williams, a fugitive from his diocese of York, was a native of
the town. He flung himself into the task of putting Conway
into a state of defence with unclerical warlike energy. The
royalists had no need to occupy Raglan by force. The
Marquess of Worcester and his son were King's men through
and through. Raglan became the royal power-house. Here
Charles sent the young Prince of Wales for safe keeping. The
Marquess poured out his wealth in support of the royal
cause.

The major moves of the Civil War inevitably took place
outside Wales. Events in Wales were bound to depend ultimately on the success or failure of the King's arms in England.
When the royalist cause prospered, as in the early years of the
war, the Parliamentary cause was on the defensive. There
was a constant ebb and flow of battle across Pembrokeshire
and Carmarthenshire as first the Parliamentarians and then
the Royalists got the upper hand. The castles in this area
changed hands rapidly as the various armies advanced and
retreated. The same could be said of the old fortresses on the
borderland in North Wales. But none of them underwent a
serious siege. The defenders no doubt always hoped that a
shift in the general course of the war would bring them easily
back again. A decisive change came over the whole fighting
front in 1645. The Parliamentarians had now thrown up
great leaders on the battle field. Cromwell's Ironsides had
already proved their worth at Marston Moor in 1644. Now
Parliament set about rebuilding their whole army on
modern lines. When this New Model Army under Sir
Thomas Fairfax met the main Royalist army at Naseby, the
issue was not in doubt. Charles's Welsh levies fought val-
iantly, but in the end the royal infantry was crushed. After
Naseby the complete ruin of the royal cause was only a
matter of time.

The King wandered disconsolately along the Welsh border country in the vain hope of raising a new army. We hear of him again at Raglan consoling himself with bowls on the trim lawn beyond the Yellow Tower of Gwent. But even loyal Wales had had enough. The King's final attempt to put an army in the field failed. His last Welsh levies were scattered at Rowton Heath outside Chester and the unhappy King is supposed to have watched from the walls. There was no more to be done in the field. Only some of the castles "like winter fruit, hung long on". They were manned by die-hard Royalists who were still prepared to hold out for honour's sake.

It was now that many of the old castles of Wales went into action for the last time. In North Wales, Ruthin held out for seven weeks. Stout-hearted Sir John Salisbury, known as Hosanau Gleison, "Old Blue Stockings", gallantly defended Denbigh until the big siege guns were brought up and there was no option but surrender. It was the same at Conway. The irresistible forces of Parliament stormed the town walls with scaling ladders, and although the castle held out, Archbishop Williams could not bear to see his native town utterly ruined. He tactfully changed sides and negotiated reasonable surrender terms. He performed the same service for Beaumaris. Caernarfon offered stronger resistance but the menace of the big guns once again did the trick.

Away in the south, Raglan prepared for a last-ditch stand. The Marquess of Worcester still had 800 men in or around the castle. Earthworks kept the besiegers at a distance, although their leader, Colonel Morgan, was an old hand at the business of attacking strong points. The fall of Oxford in June, 1646, released more men for the Raglan siege, and the garrison were "reduced to more caution and taught to lie closer". Then Parliament's most experienced military engineer, Colonel Hooper, arrived. The siege now proceeded with all the correct formal construction of trenches and parallels, and the planting of batteries ever closer to the walls. The remains of the elaborate earthworks thrown up by the attackers and defenders can still be seen just beyond

Castle Farm about a quarter of a mile north-east of the castle itself.

Colonel Hooper's guns now could play with effect upon the walls. They smashed in one side of the Pitched Stone Court. The big mortars threw 12″ "grenado" shells with powerful effect. When Sir Thomas Fairfax came down to push on the siege, the end was near. There was no Royalist army in the field which could hope to rescue the garrison. The Marquess had no option but to surrender. We have a vivid and moving account of how he and his household stood in the Great Hall and awaited Fairfax as the gates of the castle were flung open and the tumultuous rush of the besiegers flooded into the outer courtyard. The fall of Raglan meant, in effect, the end of the first Civil War, although Harlech, as usual, did not haul down the Royalist flag until March 1647.

There was one final flare-up before the castles of Wales bowed gracefully out of history. In the short-lived Second Civil War, Puritan malcontents and desperate Royalists both seized castles. Sir Nicholas Kemeys garrisoned Chepstow for the King with 120 men. Cromwell himself came down to South Wales after the field force of rebels had already been smashed at St. Fagans, outside Cardiff, by a section of the New Model Army. He called on Sir Nicholas to surrender. When Sir Nicholas refused, Cromwell moved on westward after leaving behind a regiment and enough artillery to finish the job. The heavy guns got methodically to work. Four of them battered at the curtain near Martin's Tower. The battlements were smashed and then a huge breach was made in the curtain wall. Sir Nicholas could not get his men to stand firm as the besiegers advanced. They started to run out to surrender. Sir Nicholas himself was killed.

At Pembroke, Colonel Poyer, who had previously fought strongly for Parliament and was Mayor of the town, threw out the Roundheads and provisioned the town and castle for a siege. He was joined by other prominent local Parliamentarians, including Major-General Rowland Laugharne, who had also played a distinguished part in the first Civil War. Disappointment at their reward may have had something to do with this change of allegiance. Cromwell appeared before Pembroke on May 24, 1648. He had marched fast and far and Had only his light artillery with him. This accounts for the fact that he could make no serious impression on the defence. He sent to Carmarthenshire for shot to be cast in the iron furnaces there, and tried to cut the siege short by an escalade. His men got over the town wall near the barbican but were driven out. A second attempt failed because the ladders were too short. Cromwell waited for his big guns to be sent by sea from Gloucester. All through the Civil War transporting a proper siege-train was a problem. The roads in 17th century England were still of mediaeval muddiness. Even light guns were hard to drag onto the battlefield and artillery never played a decisive part in the battles of the Civil War. The gun was essentially a siege weapon. When the big guns could eventually be got into position before the walls of a mediaeval castle, the result was not long in doubt. No amount of courage and resource could stand against them. Cromwell had already reported to the Speaker that there was discontent among the defenders of Pembroke. "We hear they mutinied about three days since; cried out 'Shall we be ruined for two or three men's pleasure? Better it were that we should throw them over the walls' ".

The big guns finally opened up and all was over. Poyer surrendered on July 11. He and two other renegades were sentenced to death. Parliament allowed them to draw lots so that only one should die. The fatal lot fell on Poyer. He was shot in Covent Garden, where he faced his death with brave dignity.

The Second Civil War forced the victors to look again at the old castles. They had proved an unexpected nuisance. With the exception of a few like Chepstow which were still found useful as arms-stores and military bases, Parliament felt that castles should be permanently put out of action - "slighted" was the word of the day. Towers should be blown up, lengths of the curtain wall demolished. No rebel would ever again have a chance of holding them against the new goverment. When Pembroke fell Cromwell lost no time in issuing orders that the more troublesome castles of Pembrokeshire should be made completely unusable. As you read the crisp note he wrote to the burgesses of Haverfordwest within days of the surrender of Pembroke, you sense that Cromwell had had more than enough of castles. They could not affect the general issue in any way but imposed a tiresome burden on the troops who had to go through the business of reducing them. Cromwell wrote to the municipal authorities of Haverfordwest that they were "forthwith to demolish the workes, walls and towers of the said castle, soe as the said castle may not be possest by the enemy, to the endangerouing of the peace of these parts"; and he added a brisk reminder that he expected immediate action. "We expect an account of your proceedings with effect in this business by Saturday . . . If a speedy course be not taken to fulfil the commands of this warrant, I shall be necessitated to consider of settling a garrison". The threat was enough. Haverfordwest was immediately "slighted"; as indeed was Pembroke.

Not every broken castle in Wales is "one of the ruins that Cromwell knocked about a bit". Some had already lost their defensive power long before the Civil War. But Parliamentary "slighting" accounts for a great deal of damage. The famous Leaning Tower of Caerphilly was probably the result of a somewhat unskilful attempt to blow up the defences. The old mediaeval walls were so strongly built that they caused endless trouble to the wreckers. Maybe that is why Caernarfon survived, although it was placed on the list for destruction. Goodrich received full attention. Saddest of all, Raglan was deliberately destroyed.

After the siege ended, Parliament ordered that "the castle, the works about it, the house and buildings were to be forthwith pulled down and demolished". The country people were summoned. They tried to knock down the Great Tower with picks, but it was far too well built for such treatment. It was undermined, the timber props set on fire and part of the wall then collapsed. The books of the library, many of them irreplaceable early Welsh manuscripts, were burnt. As the years passed, the old castle was used as a quarry, and a convenient source of ornament for the great-house which the Herbert family, now created Dukes of Beaufort, built at Badminton after the Restoration. One ducal steward plundered with such a will that he received the title of The Great Dilapidator.

But time was the greatest dilapidator of them all. For a hundred years after the Civil War castles were firmly out of favour. The men of the post-Restoration period felt that these broken walls now held bitter memories. No-one wanted to remember the miseries they represented. To the classical 18th century, castles were uncivilised Gothic memorials best left to the destructive clutches of the ivy. But as the 18th century drew to its close a more sympathetic view began to prevail. The poets cast a romantic glow over "the ivy-mantled tower", where "the moping owl doeth to the moon complain". The painters and engravers were not far behind the poets. Men like Turner and Girtin created master-pieces out of the "ivy-mantled towers". Finally Sir Walter Scott brought the Middle Ages firmly back into fashion. So much so that, when the Industrial Revolution yielded rich rewards to the new monied class, the successful industrialists felt that they had to symbolise their success by living in some sort of mediaeval castle. Even the nobility began to Gothicise their 18th century country-seats.

Just outside Bangor in North Wales, Lord Penrhyn built himself a splendid pseudo-castle on the money that flowed in from his slate quarries. It included a complete reconstruction of a Norman Square Keep, which can still create a powerful architectural effect. Later on, the Marquess of Bute, on the money from coal, inspired the remarkable remodelling of Cardiff Castle and the rebuilding of Castell Coch - probably the most elaborate and interesting scheme of this kind ever carried out in Britain.

In our own day, the castles have been valued as never before. The Department of the Environment - the heir to the old Ministry of Public Building and Works - has taken most of the greater Welsh castles into its scholarly care. We can walk on the green lawns surrounding the grey walls and let our imagination journey back into the Past. For how can we understand our turbulent Present if we are ignorant of the way our forefathers lived, felt and talked. The memory of the men who made our early history crowds in upon us as we explore the ruined halls, the towers, the broken battlements. We can see the actual spot at Flint where the unhappy Richard II, having heard Mass, went upon the walls of the castle and saw the host of his supplanter Henry Bolingbroke marching towrds him along the sea-shore and then knew he had lost his whole kingdom. We can stand in the ruined hall of Raglan and hear, in our imagination, the tramp of the stern soldiers of Fairfax as they came to confront the aged Marquess of Worcester and bring total ruin to his house. Beside the great fireplace in Carreg Cennen the watchmen must have warmed themselves as they came down from the lonely walls after their chill all night spell of duty in the days when Owain Glyn Dŵr might have come pouncing down from the North. These walls can still speak powerfully to us across the years. And with knowledge we can still recapture the delight and surprise of the poet of "Sir Gawain and the Green Knight" as he looked at a newly-built castle in the high noon of mediaeval castle-building; and we remember that the man who wrote "Sir Gawain" knew his North Wales.

"There were fair watchtowers fashioned in between, with many graceful loop-holes that shut fast. A better barbican the Knight had never looked upon. And within he saw the hall full high, set about with towers whose tall pinnacles were cunningly carved. On the roof of the towers he beheld a multitude of white chimneys that glittered as if they were chalk. And the battlements clustered so closely that it seemed as if the whole castle was carved out of paper".

It could be a vision of Conway or Caernarfon as they came fresh from the genius of the builder, Master James of St. George!

The Square Keep

Great Hall

Kitchen

Postern Gate

Guest Apartments

Chapel

Apartments

UPPER WARD

Well

Armoury

Forge and stores

Curtain-wall with Brattice

Barracks

Dry Moat

Great Gate house

Merlon

Crenel

Machicolations

Putlog Holes

Wet Moat

Turning bridge

LOWER WARD

Stables

Portcullis

Crenel with Shutters

Barbican

Draw-bridge

Allure

Tower with Brattice

Parts of a Typical Castle

A composite castle of the 13th century

THE DEVELOPMENT OF THE CASTLE

This series of photographs of details from the castles of Wales shows the stages in the growth of the castle—from the simple 'motte and bailey' to the final complexities of the concentric principle—and the change in the role of the castle after the advent of gunpowder.

a.　CARDIFF. The motte, or mound, was built by the Normans in their first invasion of Glamorgan. It is one of the highest in South Wales. The shell keep came later. Cardiff is the easiest place to see the classic 'motte and bailey' construction—the first fortified works constructed by the Norman barons as they invaded S. Wales in the 11th and early 12th centuries.

b.   CHEPSTOW. The earliest of the square keeps in S. Wales. It was built by William
Fitzosbern, Lord of Breteuil in Normandy, who was created Earl of Hereford
after the Norman Conquest. Chepstow was his base for the conquest of modern
Monmouthshire. The keep was added to in later years. The lower two stories and
the doorway, with its rounded lintel, give an excellent idea of the power of the
first square keeps in the early days of castle-building.

c. PEMBROKE. The round keep displaces the square keep. This splendid example was probably built by William Marshall, Earl of Pembroke from 1189 to 1219. This model was extensively copied in South Wales. In theory the round keep had greater defensive strength than the square one. There were no vulnerable corners to be attacked by battering rams or by undermining. This keep is 100ft. high with the top storey covered by a stone dome, against fire.

d. WHITE CASTLE. Monmouthshire. By the beginning of the 13th century the castle walls were becoming even more important than the keep. Towers were added to provide flanking fire along the circuit of the walls. The castle now consisted of an inner and an outer ward. In the elaborate reconstruction of the middle of the 13th century, the old square keep at White Castle was demolished as being of no further use to the defence.

e.   SKENFRITH. One of the "Three Castles". Together with White Castle and Grosmont, Skenfrith controlled Northern Monmouthshire. The group was always in common ownership, usually by the baron. When Skenfrith was reconstructed by Herbert de Burgh around 1220, the original wooden and earthen palisade was replaced by a stone wall with the now popular flanking towers. De Burgh, however, still retained the concept of the Round Keep. By the middle of the 13th century, a construction like Skenfrith would begin to look distinctly old-fashioned.

f.

g.

13th CENTURY ELABORATIONS. The castle became steadily more complex as the 13th century progressed. f. The Barbican at Chepstow. This was designed to break the force of the attack before it came up against the main gatehouse. g. The Gatehouse at Kidwelly. The gatehouse had now replaced the keep as the aggressive strong-point of the defence. The actual entrance was protected by two flanking towers. Above were the arches of the machicolations. h. The walls of Pembroke, showing the "crenels" with the "allure" behind. The postern gate is seen on the left near the foot of the round tower.

WELSH CASTLES. i. Ewloe in Flintshire, a few miles from the English border. The square keep was a characteristic feature of the castles built by the Welsh princes. The circuit walls were usually not provided with flanking towers. Ewloe is interesting as an example of a castle built by the Welsh which was abandoned after the Edwardian conquest. Dolwyddelan (on the opposite page), was probably built by Llywelyn the Great at the beginning of the 13th century. Again the keep remains the central feature. The upper storey battlements are a later 19th-century restoration.

j.   DOLWYDDELAN, Caernarvonshire.

Overleaf

THE DEVELOPMENT OF THE CONCENTRIC CASTLE. k. Caerphilly, the
first and still the greatest concentric castle in Wales. Note the enormous platforms
that held back the water of the moat. The inner castle is a true concentric castle in
itself. Beyond it lies the grass-covered hornwork. l. Kidwelly. Notice how the
inner ward dominates the outer in a concentric castle. m. A 19th-century
reconstruction, at Cardiff castle, of the shutters that protected archers using the
"crenels" or open spaces of the battlements. n. Rhuddlan, Edward I's principal
base for his final conquest of N. Wales. A concentric castle with a special defensive
arrangement to protect the quay on the banks of the River Clwyd.

k.   Caerphilly (above)   l   Kidwelly (belo

1. Cardiff Castle (above)   n.   Rhuddlan (below)

EDWARDIAN CASTLES. o. Caernarvon (above) shows the close relationship between the castle and the town. They were planned as mutually supporting defensive units. p. Conway town walls and the remarkable array of "garderobes" or privies along the wall. Edward I sited an important administrative building here which needed special provision. q. Cricieth. The outer and lower defensive circuit was built by Llywelyn the Great. After the conquest, Edward I built an inner ward with the characterising powerful gatehouse with the two flanking towers. He thus converted Cricieth into a true concentric castle.

Conway Town Walls and Garderobes (above)   q.   Cricieth (below)

r. RAGLAN, Monmouthshire. Raglan was planned in the middle of the 15th
century when the cannon and gunpowder had already appeared on the military
scene. The Yellow Tower of Gwent is surrounded by a moat and contains small
portholes for guns. Note the elaborate "machicolations" on the gatetowers. The
outer and inner courtyards were carefully re-modelled to conform to the new
Tudor standards of comfort and elegance. Raglan was finally wrecked in the Civil
War by the forces of Parliament.

s.   POWYS CASTLE, Monmouthshire. The original castle was the seat of the Welsh
Princes of Powys, whose territory included the valleys of the Dee and the Upper
Severn. Its history was reasonably uneventful since the Prince of Powys generally
pursued a subtle policy of plant accommodation with the powerful English Kings.
Powys was extensively re-modelled in the late 17th century, when the remarkable
terraced gardens were created and the interior rebuilt in great splendour.

t.   CHIRK CASTLE, Denbighshire. Again a castle reconstructed to suit changing times. The plan still retains the square enclosure created under Edward I, with the two corner towers reminiscent of Rhuddlan. It was extensively opened out in Tudor times, when it was granted to the Middleton family, in whose possession it still remains.

What to see in the Castles of Wales-and Where

This short gazeteer is designed simply to indicate the castles in which the various developments of the art of defence can best be studied. Most Welsh castles were continually being added to or reconstructed over many centuries. A castle like Chepstow, for example, can show features from the 11th and 13th and even the 17th centuries. Some castles will, therefore, be mentioned several times under the various headings. The gazeteer is concerned only with the castles that are basically mediaeval in date. Those open to the public at stated times are marked * (Department of the Environment) or ** (other public bodies or private individuals). Other sites are on private property and require permission to visit from the owners.

1. *Motte and Bailey Castles.* It is clearly impossible to mention every motte and bailey in Wales. There are nearly 30 in Carmarthenshire alone and Carmarthenshire is not the most "be-castled" county in Wales. Most of them are marked on the 1 inch Ordnance map and motte-hunting can be a rewarding and fascinating exercise. A day spent tracking the numerous mottes that are scattered along the valley of the Usk between Abergavenny and Brecon will teach you a great deal about the way the Normans advanced into the hills of Wales. Here is a list of a few mottes which are easily accessible or which lie on striking and important sites: ABER, at the entrance to the Menai Straits; BALA; BLAENCAMLAIS,

splendidly placed fronting the wild hills near the modern Mountain Centre about five miles south-west of Brecon; CARDIFF: CAERLEON: CRUG ERYR, in Radnorshire, where Geraldus Cambrensis stayed with Archbishop Baldwin when preaching the Third Crusade in 1188; PENCADER: RHUDDLAN*: ST CLEARS: TOMEN-Y-MUR: TRECASTLE.

In addition Gower has two ring-mottes at PENRICE and PENMAEN.

2. *Keeps*

(a) *Square Keeps*. Wales cannot show many 11th century keeps. Most of them belong to the 12th century when the Norman penetration of South and Mid Wales was in full swing. The oldest is CHEPSTOW*, built by William FitzOsbern around 1070. Other later examples are: OGMORE; COITY (much altered in the 15th century), and the noble Keep at GOODRICH*, on the Wye just over the border in Herefordshire. MONMOUTH's Great Tower is also mid-12th century work, again much altered.

(b) *Round Keeps*. South Wales contains most of these impressive structures. PEMBROKE** was the first and greatest of them. The Usk valley and its tributaries has an interesting and probably inter-related group at TRETOWER*, BRONLLYS* and SKENFRITH*. Two notable round keeps are CALDICOT** on the marshlands of the Severn in Monmouthshire and PENRICE in Gower. Two others present problems since they occur in castles built by the Welsh. One is in North Wales in Snowdonia where DOLBADARN* has a strong central round tower - most Welsh-constructed keeps were square. The other is at DINEFWR, with its strong round keep which has been compared to the great keep at Coucy in France; Sir John Rees has suggested that it might have been built, not by the Lord Rhys, but during a temporary English occupation.

(c) *Shell Keeps*. The classic example is CARDIFF**, where the keep is perched on top of one of the highest mottes in Wales. Not so well known is the smaller shell-keep at WISTON, in Pembrokeshire. The motte on which it stands is heavily overgrown, and is surrounded by a surprisingly large bailey. Wiston gets its name from Wizo, the Fleming lord of the country around the upper reaches of Milford Haven. The castle was over-run by the Welsh during the reign of Llywelyn the Last. TRETOWER** combines a shell keep with a round keep in the centre and is the only example of this form of construction in Wales.

3. The Development of the Curtain Wall. Here, WHITE CASTLE has most to show. The original circuit of the Inner Bailey was a stone wall without towers. Then, the towers were added, the old keep levelled, and the whole castle re-orientated according to the new fortification principles of the late 13th century. White Castle is also extensively moated and has a fine example of a horn-work. SKENFRITH also has a simple circuit with towers at the corners. The wall circuit was probably built in the early 13th century but there was no attempt to build an elaborate gatehouse. BRIDG-END has a simple gateway and a circuit of walls that for the most part dispenses with towers. This gateway still retains its elaborately decorated 12th century arch.

4. *Enceinte Castles.* The majority of the stone-built castles of Wales belong to the great period of castle construction which spanned the years roughly from 1270 to 1340. They, therefore, consist of one or two wards, depending on the administrative importance of the site and its defensive advantages. A castle like OYSTERMOUTH**, outside Swansea, was not the most important place in the Lordship. The builders were, therefore, content with a simple circuit around one ward, and a complex of living quarters grouped around a keep, although they added a more modern type gatehouse in the late 13th century. The gatehouse towers have subsequently been removed leaving two semi-circles of stone to puzzle modern visitors. LLAWHADEN*, built by the Bishops of St. David, to protect their lands on the Landsker (the boundary between English and Welsh Pembrokeshire) also consists of a single ward. Here the site was probably judged strong enough not to require two wards. The same may have been true of Newcastle Emlyn.

The important castle of PEMBROKE**, on the other hand, has both inner and outer wards, CHEPSTOW*, on its narrow limestone ridge has no less than three, together with a barbican. COITY*, CILGERRAN*, and CAREW** all had two wards. Although not much remains to be seen of a stone construction, CASTELL DINAS deserves a visit for its romantic site. It lies at a height of 1,476 ft. in the Black Mountains of Monmouthshire at the top of the Rhingoil valley. Its inner and outer wards were actually constructed inside an impressive Iron Age fort. The castle is claimed to stand on the highest site in England and Wales.

The "enceinte-type" castle, as it grew in complexity and ingenuity developed certain special features which can all be illustrated from the castles of Wales.

(a) *The Barbican.* CHEPSTOW* has the most complete example which protects the upper west end of the site and is almost an integral part of the castle. There are ruins of elaborate barbicans at CARREG CENNEN* and GOODRICH*. CAERPHILLY* has a series of barbicans. Some of the Edwardian period castles in North Wales, including CONWAY* and DENBIGH* also have interesting remains of their old barbicans, while a small but largely complete barbican protects the entrance to the south gateway at BEAUMARIS*.

(b) *Machicolations.* Most of the great gate-houses of the late 13th and early 14th century were well supplied with these devices. KIDWELLY* is notable, but you can also see them on the gatehouse of the sadly neglected castle of NEATH. RAGLAN* has a splendid series encircling the tops of the towers.

(c) *Posterns or Sally-Ports.* Many castles were supplied with these small easily blocked and defended side gates which allowed individuals or small parties to slip in and out of the main defences. Posterns can be seen at PEMBROKE**, CILGERRAN*, and the central castle at CAERPHILLY*. DENBIGH* has a particularly elaborate postern defended by a small barbican.

(d) *The Great Gatehouse.* The development of the gate-house until it displaced the keep as the main defensive point of the castle was the key-note of castle thinking throughout the 13th century. This development can be seen at LLAN-STEPHAN*, NEATH, KIDWELLY*, PEMBROKE** and CAERPHILLY*. The climax was reached in the Edward-ian castles of North Wales, with such formidable con-structions as the King's Gate at CAERNARFON*, with its impressive array of portcullis slots, murder holes, draw-bridge and flanking arrow slits. Equally impressive, al-though partially in ruin, is the gatehouse of DENBIGH*. Perhaps the final triumph of the gatehouse occurs at HARLECH* where it's the major part of the castle.

5. *Concentric Castles.* Here CAERPHILLY* is still the greatest in Europe, BEAUMARIS* the most perfect. RHUDDLAN* was planned as a concentric castle; CRICIETH* became one when Edward I added an Inner Ward. HARLECH* is a notable example of the application of the concentric plan to a rocky site. KIDWELLY* is semi-concentric - the builders felt that the side towards the river was sufficiently protected by a steep hill slope. GOODRICH* has an outer ward linked to its dry moat in a construction clearly following the concentric idea. ST. DONAT's, on the coast of Glamorgan, was built by Sir Peter de Stradling, who had come to Britain in the train of Otto de Grandson, Edward I's viceroy in North Wales. Sir Peter is not recorded as having been in North Wales, but it is likely that a Savoyard would be aware of the ideas of Master James, and would, therefore, be willing to use them in constructing his more modest castle in the south.

6. *Towns and Castles.* Throughout Wales, small towns grew up in the shadow of the castle walls or were deliberately created by the castle builders. The relationship between town and castle can best be studied in the great Edwardian buildings in North Wales. CAERNARFON* and, above all, CONWAY* have magnificent circuits which have few rivals in Europe. DENBIGH town walls are also closely linked

with the castle in one defensive concept. In South Wales CHEPSTOW* is the best example. PEMBROKE** walls are not complete but stretches of them can be seen on the south side of the town. KIDWELLY* walls have gone, but the earthen bank is still there, as is the stone-built gatehouse at the bottom of Castle Street. TENBY** has preserved far more, including the well-known Five Arches tower. The walls were still thought to be worth strengthening seriously in 1457 in the age of gunpowder. COWBRIDGE has a short, somewhat ignored stretch of town wall running from the church and Grammar School. The site of MONTGOMERY's circuit can be traced.

7. *Edwardian Castles.* The great ones are among the show-places of Wales and must be visited. Castles like CAER-NARVON*, CONWAY*, HARLECH*, BEAUMARIS* and RHUDDLAN* are the high peak of mediaeval castle-builder's art. Their only rivals in South Wales are CAERPHILLY* and KIDWELLY*. Between them they em-body all the tricks and devices that were known to the military architects before the age of gunpowder. Other Royal castles of the period include the interesting FLINT* and the much 'slighted' ABERYSTWYTH**. The walls of BUILTH have completely disappeared but the pattern of the wards can be distinguished among the huge grassy mounds. The ancillary castles of DENBIGH* and RUTHIN were both built under the influence of Master James of St. George. More remains of Ruthin than might be expected among the 19th century reconstruction. DENBIGH*, and its town wall is surprisingly impressive. Much less can be seen of the other castles that played such prominent parts in the troubled border-land forays of the Age of the Two Llywelyns in Flint-shire and Denbighshire. HOLT barely survives. HAWARDEN stands in the park near to the private mansion that once belonged to Mr. Gladstone. HOPE has a magnifi-cent site on a wooden rocky hill overlooking Caergwrle vill-age, but only parts of the inner ward are left. The careful ash-lar construction of the immensely thick walls must have made Hope impressive in its day. CHIRK, called by the

Welsh Castell y Waun, is still inhabited, although heavily reconstructed.

8. *Castles built by the Welsh.* The Welsh began their castle-building rather late in the day and in imitation of their Norman and English foes. They also did not have the resources to build on the scale of a Caernarfon or a Caerphilly. Nevertheless a number of Welsh-built castles have survived, particularly in North Wales. Although many of the castles in South Wales were Welsh in origin, most of them, like Dinefwr and Newcastle Emlyn, were so thoroughly rebuilt after the Edwardian wars that it is difficult to find any traces of Welsh construction in them. In North Wales, however, the Age of the Two Llywelyns was an age of castle building and some of their castles survive. Earlier Owain Gwynedd had built castles of the motte and bailey type on his borders with the Anglo-Norman lordships to the east. One of them, TOMEN Y RHODWYDD, stands at the roadside near the southern end of the Nant y Garth pass and is on a considerable scale. The stone castles built by the Llywelyns usually have a main tower embodying the concept of the keep, a secondary tower and a curtain around the site. EWLOE*, near Hawarden, is probably the best preserved of them, and was left unaltered after Edward's conquest of North Wales. CASTELL Y BERE*, in the wilds of Cader Idris, was partially reconstructed after the fall of Llywelyn the Last. The two well-known castles of Snowdonia, DOLWYDDELAN* in the Lledr valley and DOLBADARN* at Llanberis, both conform to the pattern of Ewloe; the battlements and the top of the keep of Dolwyddelan are 19th century reconstructions. Other castles built by the Llywelyn's include CASTELL CARNDOCHAN on a crag in the mountains at the end of the valley of the Dee - little remains on the site. There is somewhat more to see of the two castles built by Llywelyn the Last on his southern boundary. DOLFOR-WYN*, on the hill above the Severn at Abermule, is now in the hands of the Department of the Environment, although they have not yet started work on the site, which is somewhat inaccessible. Some excavation has been done on

CASTELL BRYN AMLWG, high on the Kerry Hill behind Newtown, where a stone-built gatehouse was uncovered among the grassy mounds. POWYS** castle, just outside Welshpool, was the seat of the ruling family of the principality of that name. It was lavishly and splendidly remodelled in the later 17th and 18th century, but little remains of mediaeval date. DINAS BRAN, outside Llangollen is a mere fragment and awaits a detailed survey before its construction can be properly studied.

9. *The Age of Gunpowder.* RAGLAN* is the finest of the 15th century castles of Wales. Here you can see the first attempts of the castle builder to come to terms with the new conditions imposed by gunpowder. NEWPORT* in Monmouthshire was almost rebuilt in the mid-15th century, and possesses an interesting water-gate. Smaller fortified manor houses can be seen at TRETOWER* in Breconshire and at OXWICH* and WEOBLEY in Gower. BEAUPRE*, in the Vale of Glamorgan is somewhat later in date. Castles remodelled and "opened up" to adopt them to the promise of the Tudor peace at CAREW** and LAUGHARNE, with RAGLAN*, once again, offering an impressive example of the new-style domestic architecture which was transforming the Castle into the Great House. RAGLAN is therefore, a fitting end to this short survey of the Castles of Wales.

Further Reading

There is a full and fascinating literature on the history and structure of the castles of Britain. The pioneer scientific survey goes back to 1884 when G.T. Clark published his two volumes on "Mediaeval Architecture in England". This was a landmark in the study of British castle building, for in 1884 Wales was included with England without apology. The even earlier works of Viollet-le-Duc (1879) in their English translations are now difficult to come by. His volumes have been out-dated to some extent by modern scholarship, but the writing is vivid and descriptive and can still stir the imagination. For greater understanding of our military architectural heritage we must naturally now turn to more modern works. The late B.H.J. O'Neil, former Chief Inspector of Ancient Monuments, wrote an excellent short introduction to the subject entitled "Castles" (H.M.S.O.). His "Castles and Cannon" is also useful. D.F. Renn in his "Norman Castles in Britain" (Humanities Press 1969) presents a full list of the castles which contain clear evidence of Norman or Plantagenet construction. It is especially useful in tracing the smaller castles of Wales. A short popular survey of the field is contained in W. Douglas Simpson's "Castles in Britain" (Batsford, 1966).

The Department of the Environment, on behalf of the Welsh Office, publishes excellent monographs for nearly all the castles in its care and these can usually be bought on the site. More detailed architectural descriptions of individual castles are published in the County Inventories published by the Royal Commission on Ancient and Historic Monuments in Wales, where these have been completed. The documentary background to the building of the Edwardian Castles is given in "The Kings Works" (H.M.S.O., 1963).

Some useful and easily obtained studies giving the general background to castle building are "The Norman Achievement" by Professor David C. Douglas (Fontana, 1972) and the Fontana Economic History of Europe - "The Middle Ages" (ed. Carlo M. Cipolla, 1972). Much fascinating information about mediaeval building methods is to be found in "Building in England down to 1540" (O.U.P. 2nd edn. 1967).

When we come to the Welsh historical background, however, we are in a difficulty. There is no volume that can give the newcomer a narrative of Welsh history from the Beginnings to the close of the Middle Ages. The great classic work in this field is Sir J. E. Lloyd's "History of Wales", but it stops at the death of Llywelyn the Last and was, after all, first published in 1911. There have been vast changes in our view of Welsh mediaeval history since then. Professor A.H. Dodd has published a short survey but it naturally does not have the space to go into details. For those with some previous knowledge of the subject there is the excellent first volume of "Wales Through the Ages" (Christopher Davies, 1959) a collection of radio talks given by experts on the main aspects of the history of Wales prior to the 16th century. With the 16th century, we have Professor David Williams' well-known "History of Modern Wales" which is invaluable for the Tudors and the Civil War period. There is, also, Professor Glanmor Williams' masterpiece, "The Welsh Church from Conquest to Reformation" (U.W.P. 1962) which is so much more than an ecclesiastical history.

For separate aspects of the subject, however, there are numerous studies which are helpful. There are two volumes in the Heinemann series of Regional Archaeologies which give useful short surveys of the prehistory of North and

South Wales in Roman times edited by Katherine Watson (1965) and for the similar period in South Wales by C. Houlder and W.H. Manning (1966). For anyone wishing to see Roman Wales in the field the indispensable work is the late V.E. Nash Williams's "The Roman Frontier in Wales" (U.W.P.) as revised by Michael G. Jarrett in 1969. For the Dark Ages the stimulating "Arthur's Britain" by Leslie Alcock gives a vivid survey of the present state of our knowledge of a dark subject and Professor E. G. Bowen's "The Settlement of the Celtic Saints in Wales" has long been essential reading.

Coming to later times Professor W. Rees' "South Wales and the March 1284-1415", gives a survey of the social background but it was first published in 1924. Professor Rees has also produced an invaluable Historical Atlas of Wales (Cardiff 1951) which should be in the hands of everyone starting to take an interest in Welsh History. Professor Glanmor Williams has provided a popular history of the Glyn Dŵr revolt (Clarendon Biographies 1965)

For recent publications consult the latest edition of the comprehensive "Bibliography of the History of Wales" published by the University of Wales Press. A subscription to the Welsh Historical Review, again published by U.W.P., will allow the student to keep abreast of the progress in Welsh historical research. New ideas are constantly altering many of our long-established views of the history of Wales in the Middle Ages.

Finally, "The Flowering of the Middle Ages", edited by Joan Evans (Thames and Hudson, 1966) is a survey of all aspects of mediaeval life, including that of the castle builders, by experts in each field. It is expensive but it is worth buying for the splendid array of reproductions of mediaeval painting and manuscripts and for its photographs of some of the great architectural masterpieces of mediaeval Europe. Looking at the astonishing works they left behind them can sometimes bring us closer to our mediaeval ancestors than whole volumes of learned comment.

Welsh Words and Place Names

Abaty: *Abbey*
Aber: *river mouth, confluence*
Abergwaun: *Fishguard*
Aberhonddu: *Brecon*
Abermaw, Bermo: *Barmouth*
Abertawe: *Swansea*
Aberteifi: *Cardigan*
Ab, ap: *the son of*
Afon: *river*
Arglwydd: *lord*
Bach: *small*
Ban (pl. bannau): *high place, summit*
Betws: *oratory, chapel*
Blaen: *upper reaces or head of a valley or river*
Bran: *crow*
Bras: *rich, large*
Brenin: *king*
Bro: *lowland, vale*
Bron: *breast of a hill*
Bryn: *hill*
Bryste: *Bristol*
Bwlch: *pass*
Bychan: *short*
Cadair: *chair*
Cae: *field*
Caer: *fort (also Chester)*
Caerfyrddin: *Carmarthen*
Caerdydd: *Cardiff*
Caergybi: *Holyhead*
Cantref: *a hundred (division of land)*
Carn: *heap of stone*
Carreg (p-. cerrig): *stone*
Casgwent: *Chepstow*
Casllwchwr: *Loughor*
Castell: *castle*
Castell Nedd: *Neath*
Castell Newydd Emlyn: *Newcastle Emlyn*
Castell y Waun: *Chirk*
Cefn: *back, ridge*
Clawdd: *bank, dyke*
Cleddau: *swords*
Coch: *red*
Craig: *rock, crag*
Crib: *comb, a narrow ridge*
Croes: *cross*
Croesoswallt: *Oswestry*
Crug: *mound*
Crughywel: *Crickhowel*
Cwmwd: *Commote, an administration area*
Cwrt: *court*
Cydweli: *Kidwelly*
Cymro: *Welshman*

Da: *good*
Dau: *two*
Dewi: *David*
Dinbych y Pysgod: *Tenby*
Dinas: *fort, city*
Dol: *meadow*
Drws: *door*
Du: *black*
Dwr: *water*
Dyffryn: *valley*
Efail: *smithy*
Eglwys: *church*
Emrys: *Ambrosius*
Erw: *acre*
Esgair: *ridge*
Ffair: *fair*
Fflur: *flower*
Ffordd: *road*
Ffos: *ditch, trench*
Ffridd: *mountain pasture*
Garth: *enclosure, hill*
Glan: *bank shore*
Glas: *green*
Glyn: *glen, valley*
Gorsedd: *throne, bardic order*
Grug: *heather*
Gwaun: *meadow*
Gwrecsam: *Wrexham*
Gwig: *wood*
Gwrtheyrn: *Vortigern*
Gwyddelod: *Irishmen*
Hafod: *summer dwelling*
Hafren: *Severn*
Hen: *old*
Hen Dy Gwyn Ar Daf: *Whitland*
Hendre: *established settlement*
Henffordd: *Hereford*
Heol: *road*
Hir: *long*
Iago: *James*
Iarll: *earl*
Isaf: *lowest*
Llam: *leap*
Llan: *church*
Llanandras: *Presteign*
Llanbedr Pont Stephan: *Lampeter*
Llanelwy: *St. Asaph*
Llanfair ym Muallt: *Builth*
Llech: *slate*
Llethr: *slope*
Llety: *lodgings*
Lloer: *moon*
Llwybr: *path*
Llwyn: *grove*
Llyn: *lake*

Llys: *hall, court*
Mab: *son*
Maen: *stone*
Maenor: *manor*
Maes: *field*
Mawn: *peat*
Mawr: *big*
Melin: *mill*
Melyn: *yellow*
Min: *edge, bank*
Moel: *bare hill*
Môr Hafren: *Bristol Channel*
Môr: *sea*
Morfa: *bog, sea-marsh*
Mur: *wall*
Mynach: *monk*
Mynydd: *mountain*
Nanhyfer: *Nevern*
Nant: *brook, stream*
Neuadd: *hall*
Newydd: *new*
Odyn: *kiln*
Oer: *cold*
Ogof: *cave*
Olaf: *last*
Onnen (pl. onn): *ash*
Pandy: *Fulling-mill*
Pant: *hollow, valley*
Parc: *park*
Pen: *top, head*
Penfro: *Pembrokeshire*
Pentref: *village*
Penybont: *Bridgend*
Plaid: *party*
Plas: *mansion*
Pont: *bridge*
Pont Faen: *Cowbridge*
Porth: *port*
Pren: *wood*
Pump: *five*
Pwll: *pool*
Rhaeadr: *waterfall*
Rhandir: *district*
Rhedyn: *bracken*
Rhiw: *hill*
Rhos: *moor, plain*
Rhwng: *between*
Rhyd: *ford*

Saesneg: *English language*
Saeth: *arrow*
Sais: *Englishman*
Sant: *saint*
Sarn: *causeway*
Sir: *County*

Mon: *Anglesey*
Brycheiniog: *Breconshire*
Caernarfon: *Caernarvonshire*
Ceredigion (Aberteifi): *Cardiganshire*
Sir Gar (Caerfyrddin): *Carmarthenshire*
Sir Ddinbych: *Denbighshire*
Y Fflint: *Flintshire*
Morgannwg: *Glamorgan*
Meirionydd: *Merioneth*
Mynwy: *Monmouthshire*
Maldwyn: *Montgomeryshire*
Penfro: *Pembrokeshire*
Maesyfed: *Radnorshire*

Taren: *knoll, rock*
Teg: *fair*
Tir: *land*
Tomen: *mound*
Traeth: *beach*
Tre, tref: *town, home*
Y Dre Newydd: *Newtown*
Treffynnon: *Holywell*
Trefyclawdd: *Knighton*
Tri: *three*
Trum: *ridge*
Ty: *House*
Ty Ddewi: *St. David's*
Uchaf: *highest*
Undeb: *union, religious denomination*
Urdd: order
Y: *the*
Y Bont Faen: *Cowbridge*
Y Gelli: *Hay*
Y Trallwng: *Welshpool*
Yr Wyddgrug: *Mold*
Ynys: *island*
Ysbyty: *hospital*
Ysgol: *school*
Ystrad: *vale*

Terms used in describing castles

Adulterine Castle   A castle built without a royal licence.

Allure   Also called the wall-walk. The flat walk on top of the curtain wall, protected by the battlements.

Arrow-slit   A narrow aperture in a castle wall or tower, designed to allow the defenders to fire their cross bows or long bows. Some arrow-slits had an "oelitte" or round opening at the base and apex

Ashlar   Regularly dressed masonry blocks.

Bailey   Ward or courtyard. A defensive circuit.

Barbican   The outer defences before the main gateway, sometimes placed on the far side of a moat or dry ditch.

Bastion   A projecting wall or tower.

Berm   The level ground between the base of the curtain and the inner edge of the ditch or moat.

Brattices   Also termed hoardings or hoards. Wooden galleries supported by beams projecting from the battlements to overlook the base of the tower or curtain walls. Could either be permanent, or erected to meet an emergency.

Concentric   Describing a castle with a high inner circuit enclosed by a lower outer one.

Constable   The governor of a castle.

Corbel   A projection from the wall designed to support a gallery or any stone structure.

Crenel   The open side of the battlements. A royal licence to crenelate meant permission to build a castle.

Curtain   The stone wall enclosing the baileys, or wards, of a castle.

Donjon	A Great Tower, either round or square, which was the last resort of the defenders.
Drawbridge	A wooden bridge leading to the gateway and raised by ropes or chains.
Embrasure	An opening in a wall.
Enceinte	The circuit enclosed by the curtain walls.
Forebuilding	A building attached to a square Norman keep, which held the stairway to the entrance.
Garderobe	Privy or latrine.
Hall	The main room in the castle, used for great formal occasions.
Hoards	See Brattices.
Hornwork	Earthwork, usually in a wet moat, defending the secondary gatehouse.
Keep	See Donjon.
Machicolations	Openings between corbels, allowing the garrison to throw down missiles.
Merlons	The solid sections of the battlements.
Moat	Deep ditch around the curtain. Dry or filled with water.
Motte	Mound of earth on which a wooden tower could be built.
Murder Holes	Or 'meurtrieres'. Holes above the entrance passage in a gateway, through which the defenders could hurl down missiles.
Penthouse	Also Pentise. A lean-to.
Portcullis	A wooden grille shod with iron and let down with chains to close the gatehouse entrance.
Postern	A side or secondary doorway. Also termed a sally-port.

Putlogs	Beams for supporting overhanging galleries on curtain walls or towers. They were inserted in specially made putlog holes.
Rainures	The beams with chains attached for hoisting a drawbridge.
Shell-keep	The stone circuit replacing the palisades on the top of a motte.
Solar	The private apartments of the lord or custodian of the castle; in early days adjacent to the hall.
Turning-bridge	A wooden bridge pivoted around an axle, and worked by a counterweight. Common in the Edwardian and early 14th-century castles.
Ward	A courtyard or bailey.

INDEX